IT'S IN THE CARDS

IT'S IN THE CARDS

Consumer Credit and the American Experience

Lloyd Klein

 PRAEGER

Westport, Connecticut
London

Library of Congress Cataloging-in-Publication Data

Klein, Lloyd, 1951–
    It's in the cards : consumer credit and the American experience /
    Lloyd Klein.
        p.   cm.
    Includes bibliographical references and index.
    ISBN 0–275–95757–8 (alk. paper)
        1. Consumer credit—Social aspects—United States.   2. Consumer
    credit—United States.   3. Credit cards—United States.   I. Title.
    HG3756.U54K59   1999
    332.7'43—dc21   97–9177

British Library Cataloguing in Publication Data is available.

Library of Congress Catalog Card Number: 97–9177
ISBN: 0–275–95757–8

First published in 1999

Praeger Publishers, 88 Post Road West, Westport, CT 06881
An imprint of Greenwood Publishing Group, Inc.
www.praeger.com

Printed in the United States of America

The paper used in this book complies with the
Permanent Paper Standard issued by the National
Information Standards Organization (Z39.48–1984).

10 9 8 7 6 5 4 3 2 1

Contents

Preface

Consumer credit is a mainstay of our society. Individuals from every social class position and virtually every occupation or profession accept debt as a way of life. Credit cards are freely marketed on college campuses and at public events. The proferred plastic cards permit the acquisition of many previously unaffordable goods and services.

If we can accept the notion that there is nothing more powerful than an economic idea whose time has come, then consumer credit and financial debt are indicative of the current state of our society. We live fast-paced lives, obtaining airline tickets or other high-priced items on consumer credit and settling the debt at a later point. The middle-class lifestyle is made more attainable through the constant marketing and consumer acceptance of merchandise and provided services. Consumer activity fueled by plastic no longer bears the same stigma as it did for generations preceding and immediately after World War II.

A thorough analysis of consumer credit goes beyond the mere acknowledgment of credit card availability and debt. We must answer questions regarding where the credit card concept originated, why credit cards are a part of many individuals everyday transactions; and the ultimate impact of consumer credit on American lives. The research scope of this study examines the relationship between consumer credit social control mechanisms and the imposition of cultural values. The primary research focus assumes that the utilization of consumer credit since World War II has been accompanied by increased institutional controls associated with a substantial cultural impact on American life. Influence associated with widespread banking dissemination of credit cards, along with their subsequent marketing and distribution through rationalized business practices, accompanied American consumer acceptance of credit as a normalized social activity. The extent in which credit cards were marketed as a product and chosen consumers were designated as recipients of the financial instruments is a major element in subsequent cultural change. Subsequent credit industry control over spending limits dictated the quantity of consumer activity and the spending thresholds. Financial industry power even included the determination of standards justifying the restoration of creditworthy individuals during post-bankruptcy periods.

Cultural values are seen as status formations stemming from economic development. Product distribution is dependent on previously assessed or changing consumer desires. Credit cards, installment credit, and other consumer credit instruments facilitated the development of the service sector from the preindustrial stage through the post-Fordist (or postmodern) dependence on niche or planned marketing.

The cultural impact of consumer credit is connected with the ascendence of marketing and cultural change. Consumers have accepted credit cards as instruments for the facilitated acquisition of available goods and services. The rise of consumer debt and industrial forgiveness of accumulated debt has gained acceptance among the business sector because sustained consumer activity is absolutely necessary for the continued sustenance of the marketplace. Consumers accept the premise, along with the credit services facilitating the purchase of various commodities. The overall analysis is divided into seven chapters. Chapter 1 introduces the social significance of consumer credit and the conceptual underpinning forming the ensuing analysis. Chapter 2 focuses on the developed post-Fordist tendencies within American society during the period after World War II through the early 1990s. Post-Fordist developments were accompanied by the diversification of consumer products and the increased distribution of consumer credit instruments facilitating the acquisition of those products. Chapter 3 examines the experiential realm; where, the service sector offers diverse niche marketing of specific products and experiences attainable through the utilization of consumer credit. Some of the experiences discussed in the chapter include telephone sex, fantasy suites, Disney theme parks, and Las Vegas.

Subsequent chapters elaborate on consumer credit and the development of credit card acceptance among the general populace. Chapter 4 analyzes the role of advertising in promoting the cultural utility of consumer credit.

Chapter 5 examines the retail credit sector. A socio-historical view of product distribution demonstrates how credit cards and installment plans have facilitated the development of department stores and the newly evolving forms of product distribution through shopping malls and home shopping services.

Chapter 6 offers an analysis of bankruptcy and the socio-cultural changes associated with debt forgiveness and the facile acceptance of bankruptcy as a way of life for many people. Lastly, Chapter 7 emphasizes the criteria associated with consumer bankruptcy and changing business interpretation of creditworthy status following consumer debt relief. The credit-granting cycle offers renewed hope amid a society awash in ongoing debt accumulation. Implications of the final results provide a glimpse of a materialist society stressing the oft-quoted slogan "You have to be in it to win it." The prize is a lifestyle associated with cultural gratification and certain social status.

Acknowledgments

Numerous individuals provided indispensable assistance in the shaping and the culmination of the original research. The input of several academic advisers was particularly instrumental in facilitating completion of the research analysis. I owe a huge debt of gratitude to Dr. Charles Winick for having faith in me and this project. Dr. Raymond Franklin provided considerable help through his patience and willingness to read materials. The wait stretched over ten years but I hope that the final product justified Professor Franklin's expectations.

Dr. Michael Brown made noteworthy contributions through his support over the last 15 years including introducing me to Joseph Bensman and presenting me with various constructive ideas during the early development of the current project.

My eternal gratitude goes to the late Professors Joseph Bensman and Robert Lekachman. Professor Bensman helped shape the initial theme, title, and overall perspective of the project. Additionally, he provided me with a strong role model that will always guide my professional career. Robert Lekachman was another important influence in the conceptualization of the thesis project. He offered encouragement and constructive ideas at an early phase. I will never forget Professor Lekachman's optimistic disposition despite his terminal illness.

Many colleagues offered helpful advice and encouragement throughout the long gestation period: the late Alfred McClung Lee, Hylan Lewis, Lindsay Churchill, Herb Danzger, and Shela Van Ness, Joan Luxenburg, Frank Cullen, Susan Herrick, Richard Quinney, Hal Pepinsky, Martin Schwartz, and Stuart Hills, among many others. A special note of thanks goes to Donal MacNamara and the late Edward Sagarin for their special support of my scholarly efforts and words of encouragement when they were most needed. A note of appreciation goes to the late Louis Narcez, for his concern and his belief in my abilities. I learned a lot about personal priorities, endurance, and the real meaning of my life through his courageous example.

I must also acknowledge Jennifer Beaumont, Robyn Goldsteyn, Steve Gorelick, Donal Malone, John Reilly, and the late Tom Stafford for their significant support. Steve Lang deserves special recognition for his assistance beginning with a 1990 dissertation seminar and up through the present time.

A note of appreciation must also go to various colleagues. I acknowledge the support of Thomas Edwards, Nancy Oley, and other colleagues at Medgar Evers College. Their economic support through consistent adjunct teaching assignments and overall encouragement helped sustain a long period of research and writing.

I particularly want to acknowledge the support and enthusiasm of my family during the research and writing stages. Their understanding and caring sustained the long-term effort.

Finally, the real "stars" of this research are the consumer credit industry and the various subsidiary components involved in the distribution of credit (or charge) cards and promotion of consumer credit. Numerous individuals engaged in the marketing, security, retailing, and consumer screening aspects of consumer credit were instrumental in providing important information. The foregoing analysis would have been impossible without their inestimable assistance. Subsequent interpretations and conclusions are the responsibility of this author.

1

Consumer Credit as a Social Control Mechanism

Consumer dependence on credit is an accepted part of everyday life. In fact, consumer credit has become a signifier in one's "rite of passage." Consumer credit privileges awarded to a college student or person undertaking his or her first job are an indication of credentialed status. A person is almost a nonentity until he or she establishes an ongoing credit history. Receipt of an initial credit account is essentially a form of formal economic status recognition.

Consumers are implicitly told that credit privileges facilitate the increasingly complex choices within their lives. A myriad combination of complex choices arises when individuals seek out distinctive status in a society offering various recreational and professional lifestyles.[1] Nonaccessibility of consumer credit limits consumer utilization of various services or recreational conveniences. Renting an automobile, making hotel reservations or cashing a check are dependent on consumer credit availability. "Leaving home without it" is almost surely an invitation for risking nonperson status among members of the economic community.[2]

These observations are grounded within academic parameters. Although this study will treat consumer credit as a cultural development dependent on economic systems,[3] the reader must recognize that consumer credit and the resulting debt are often approached from economic, political, and psychological perspectives.[4] Such analyses are taken into consideration as this study transcends the boundaries of traditional economic analysis with an extensive consideration of post-fordism and cultural influence.[5] The end product incorporates varied consumer options and the creation of niche marketing or diversification. Harvey (1989), uses the term "flexible accumulation" as a process facilitating the expansion of consumer credit utilization.

RESEARCH THESIS AND THEORETICAL FOCUS

This study considers consumer credit within a framework of creating social control through implicit and explicit controls on the consumption of material and experiential social products. Our everyday lives are controlled through options created for leisure-time activities.[6] Social experience is transformed into a consumer product tied to everyday acceptance of cultural alternative. Tourism and subsequent escapism are easily asessed through consumer credit and are readily offered by attractions like Las Vegas, Disneyland, Disney World and Epcot Center (Experimental Prototype Community of Tomorrow). These are among the sites analyzed in our discussion.[7]

This study explicitly examines the relationship between consumer credit, social control mechanisms, and the imposition of cultural values. These factors combine in the elaboration of the following research statement: The utilization of consumer credit since World War II has been accompanied by increased economic control associated with a substantial cultural impact on American life. Cultural values and status formation stem from extensive economic development in a social system dependent on capital-intensive product distribution.[8] Product distribution is increasingly dependent on assessing or changing consumer desires.[9] Labor-intensive workplace innovations (e.g., backroom systems for crediting and debiting credit card accounts) support capital-intensive investment in complex computerized record-keeping systems.[10]

The service sector takes on added significance as the postindustrial economic phase shifts into a post-Fordist (or postmodern) form. Continually shifting technical planning emphasizes enhanced expansion through niche marketing.[11]

Manufacturing is reindustrialized through elaborated conceptual thinking from within marketing planners. The resultant product fuels the economic marketplace with an accommodation toward consumer desires or anticipated buying preferences.

Consumer credit plays a more subtle but significant social role in the cultural framework of American society. There is an implicit interrelationship between the planned marketing of specific products and a specific population with economic purchasing ability through acquisition of consumer credit. The elaboration of a heavily rationalized financial operation into an accounting system for measuring indebtedness incurred in everyday life is a significant development. The indicated financial aspects are interlinked with denied opportunity for particular lifestyles as created by the absence of credit privileges. Several larger questions are posed explaining such developments; subsequent analysis and discussion consider the development of consumer credit instruments (particularly credit cards), why consumer credit developed in these forms, and the cultural impact of consumer credit on American society.

Cultural analyses formulated by Lefebvre (1971), Marcuse (1965), Adorno (1973), and other derivatives of the Frankfurt school equate capitalist society with induced paranoia.[12] The framework of this study does not assume the existence of a conspiracy or deliberate attempt at "seducing the masses" (see Ewen, 1976). Unfortunately, the former statement is not provable within the guidelines of available fiscal or anecdotal evidence. Sociological analysis can more definitively track the development of the consumer credit system as incorporated within specific expectations regarding the attainment of consumer goods and a related lifestyle facilitated by material or nonmaterial artifacts. Overall analysis in successive pages starts with the assumption that the consumer credit structure succeeded because the groundwork was laid by an ongoing acculturation process.

Historical, ideological, and technological developments were instrumental in paving the way for the dissemination of consumer culture. Historical developments incorporate the rise of consumer credit and the influence of important financial institutions.[13] Ideological changes in consumer acceptance of credit cards and installment debt are directly linked with the desire for symbolic goods in a competitive society.[14] Lastly, technological advances facilitated the convenience of immediately obtaining cash or credit at the point of purchase.[15] An extensive consideration of the evolutionary encroachment of consumer credit systems on everyday life is incorporated in this and several subsequent chapters.

Consumer credit is an economic force carrying important social control dimensions. Cultural expectations connected with rewards for good payment records and sanctions for violating creditor expectations are important in this regard. The explicit promotion of consumer credit and subsequent punishment for nonconformity with creditor expectations emerges as a significant dialectical relationship. On the one hand, our lives benefit greatly from the privileges of acquiring needed products without instant financial responsibility. We can travel, purchase household appliances, or seek out needed cash for gambling at racetracks and casinos. These conveniences enhance our immediate daily lives. Individuals can live spontaneously and fulfill their momentary desires.

On the other hand, acceptance of these financial privileges does carry an important human cost. Consumer credit can potentially control our lives. The impact of social control emerges when consumers must choose between accepting the immediate benefits of consumer credit or accepting explicit limitations on our everyday choices when credit is unavailable.[16]

Social control, in the form of consumer credit, sets an agenda for the disposal of newly generated material affluence. Individual choice is dependent upon the supply of available goods and the demand for specific items. Consumers apply personal earnings toward the purchase of commodities intended for the economic absorption of discretionary (or surplus) income. The institutional influences can then produce unanticipated consequences beyond product acquisition or consumption.

Social control emerges when consumers must decide whether to accept credit usage as a component of everyday life. Consumers are faced with a dilemma dictating whether conformity (or keeping up with the Joneses) is more important than maintaining individual autonomy. The effects may have been produced through calculation, but not specifically designed, under the auspices of industrial producers. The intent of industrial producers or the financial community was oriented toward consumer control for economic gain.

The final effects of cultural influence either facilitate the effectively planned consumer behavior as created by the credit industry or produce unintended and disastrous economic results. For example, one argument claims that consumer bankruptcy is positive as a control upon extending too much consumer credit or negative as counterproductive for economic growth. If we accept this premise, then bankruptcy is a built-in social barometer for indicating failure of credit allocation systems or an a weakened economic system. Judging the negative or positive qualities of these consequences is a matter best left for economists. A sociological analysis can best evaluate human motivation and the resolution of problems resulting from social choice.

In essence, we must choose between active participation within the socio-economic system or exclusion from various social strata. Veblen's (1899/1983) notion of conspicuous consumption, wherein consumers sacrifice practicality for appearances, is an essential element within this choice. Consumer credit does carry potential liabilities. Some social critics claim that economic obligations bind consumers into the social system. This process can create social control. Consumers are faced with the contradictory Durkheimian dilemma of accepting integration into a network of social economic control, while, at the same time, sacrificing a certain degree of autonomy (Durkheim, 1910/1964).

Application of this principle is readily seen when we view consumer credit as a mechanism for tying individuals into the economic system. Normative economic behavior is awarded with more credit and implied social approval. Limitations of this approval are indicated when persons accepting consumer credit and its benefits fail in reimbursing the creditor and fulfilling the contractual promise. Alternately, individuals rejecting consumer credit are also perceived as aberrant. Consumer credit is marketed as a normative part of everyday life. Individuals not accepting consumer credit are viewed as atypical.

The inevitable effects of a debtor/creditor relationship may have been produced through calculation, but not specifically designed, under the auspices of industrial producers. The intent of industrial producers may have been control for economic gain. However, the final results are sometimes overly effective or produce unintended results. Consequences of an ongoing continuum dictate the supply of consumer credit and how businesses handle the eventual consequences. For example, one argument claims that consumer bankruptcy is a positive control upon extending too much consumer credit and negative as counterproductive for economic balance. Social effect of bankruptcy and its connotations are examined at a later stage of this study.

SIGNIFICANCE OF THE CONSUMER CREDIT INDUSTRY

The consumer credit industry is an important aspect of American life. Goods and services are provided by industrial firms. The advent of a post-industrial society follows from the need for keeping account of the distribution and sale of available products. Consumers can purchase these products (or commodities) through pre-existing credit arrangements. A market for material commodities is developed through calculated projection of likely consumer wants or needs. The products are introduced into the marketplace and advertising publicity is subsequently directed toward a particular market segment. Advertising efforts are correlated with the availability of product distribution networks and foreseen prospect of consumers purchasing the particular product.

Products are alternately introduced when the active market demand for an item warrants fulfilling general consumer satisfaction or the specific satisfaction of the aforementioned market segment. These marketing decisions are inevitably linked with the relationship between wants and needs. Leiss (1978), Bell (1976b) and others explored these categories. These social researchers implicitly agreed that an object (or commodity) is a "want" when desired by a segment of the population or the whole society. For example, particular types of designer clothing, automobiles, or electronic equipment (e.g., video cassette recorders) may initially emerge as a desired object (or want). These things may subsequently become perceived as needs when people transform their existence into an absolute individual necessity. The overall process eventually takes on a life of its own in dictating available social choices and the marketing of social status.

The overall process may eventually spin out of control when the marketplace cannot fulfill particular consumer needs/wants or consumers exceed their economic debt capabilities. Bankruptcy is discussed as both an end of the process for some consumers and a new beginning for others. However, the reader must realize that the mechanical elements of the consumer credit system obscure a more important social function. The importance of consumer credit as a method of control through shaped cultural values and economic symbolism will form the basis for a more specialized analysis.

INDIVIDUAL CHARACTER STRUCTURE AND CONSUMER BEHAVIOR

Character structure and social control measures remain a constant theme stemming from Weber through more contemporary social writers.[17] An understanding of the Neo-Marxist perspective is essential for understanding how the economy has shifted from a post-industrial service oriented system into a scramble to create and exploit new cultural options. Individual identity is an important component explaining the recontextualization (or almost ad hoc reorganization) of socio-economic products offered consumers through entrepreneurial planning).

Products or intended theme park ventures are based upon images or environmental structuring enabling consumer expression of social preference. These culturally based and ever-shifting consumer interests are taken into account by Faith Popcorn and other trendy futurists when corporate planners contemplate new consumer products.[18]

Neo-marxists still insist on grounding the cultural process within the market economy. According to O'Connor (1982), capitalism is predicated upon the drive for individual identity. Entrepreneurs market consumer (or wage) goods and industrial (or capital) goods. Consumers are provided various personal options through a multitude of available commodities. The imperative for expressing individualism (Veblen, 1899/1983), terms this conspicuous consumption or invidious emulation) results in a divide and conquer effect. People are socially alienated from each other and the forces of the state.

The structure of the state is subsequently weakened under the burden of citizen and industrial demands for protection and miscellaneous benefits. Thus, the increased cost of the consumption basket (or sum total of costs for these services) reduces surplus profits generated by the capitalist apparatus. A chapter on retail outlets elaborates on the role of marketing the promotion of commodities and the creation of alienation. The entire process results in an imbalance between consumer and capitalist needs. Capitalists can produce consumer or industrial goods. Expansion of industrial capacity is curtained by manufacturers in favor of emphasizing production of consumer goods. This imbalance can upset the relationship between the promotion of capitalist profits and the broadening of the consumer market.

Why are capitalists willing to accept this unfavorable exchange? There are two explanations grounding the preceding material with the more specific thesis theme. These explanations attribute alienation and purposeful conditioning with the advent of consumerism. First, financial community members are insisting that consumer behavior acts as an antidote for the alienation of the working class. Workers feel unfulfilled and seek diversion in their everyday lives. Laborers demand more compensation in the form of wages and leisure time. Additionally, workers demand more consumer goods (in a process that Marx (1860/1967) would term the production of fetishist attitudes).

This desire is originally instilled by the capitalist system as a mechanism for inducing labor participation and is a reflection of individual perceptions. More specifically, the role of advertising in producing an agenda for consumer choices and an 'antidote' for alienation is a constant feature within an industrialized society. Ewen (1976) was correct in assuming that consumer culture arises out of a need for seeking personal comfort in pressurized domestic and work environments. Consumers buy the goods and services provided by capitalist business interests. Manufacturers must sell the available goods and services in realizing an eventual profit. However, consumers will not buy durable goods or the experiences offered by Las Vegas or Disney World unless the products offer an intrinsic reward.

Consumers are manipulated by shifting social standards. Consumer debt evolves into a way of life. Alienative effects are assuaged through invention of 'Disneyland' and its offshoots over the last thirty five years. One's credit card or line of credit provides an access for products marketed through advertising and offered as cultural alternatives.

Purposeful conditioning is the second explanation addressed in this section. Acceptance of consumer credit, degree of spending behavior, and consequences from excessive abuses are promoted and controlled by the consumer credit industry. The credit industry is faced with a two pronged dilemma. First, it must stimulate enough demand in assuring financial profits from sales, credit card annual fees, and installment payments. Second, it must deal with some overzealous customers rendered out of control through enthusiastic acceptance of these credit privileges. The degree of reward through extended credit lines or punishment exacted with denied credit privileges is determined within constant industrial reevaluations.

A discussion of credit report information dissemination within the final chapter brings these points into a more comprehensive framework. A transformation from "wants" to "needs" is the result of an implicitly intrusive social process. Marxist perceptions employed in this analysis assert that the industrial sector imposes more authoritative control than it can legitimately justify. Habermas (1971) and others claim that this autonomy is really more indicative of manipulatively pre-selected product choices rather than directly determined through public demand.

The social dynamics of supply and demand, market rationalization and social control are a few of the considerations accounting for these trends. One of the contributions of this thesis is a formulation of social control measures and relative stigma attributed to particular customers. Consumer credit functions as a credentialing device that legitimates status attainment of the credit holders. Deviant classification can subsequently emerge out of these criteria. These credentials are capable of producing social approval or invoking the stigmatizable/stigmatized potential (Goffman, 1959). Social standing can shift in accordance with official recognition or negative sanctioning.

Throughout this process, great importance is placed upon the formulation of normative values and shifts between consumer credit as a proactive development or detriment. Criteria constituting social normalcy shift according to the mores associated with the relative stage of that society. Which is more desirable—the prudent persons rejecting consumer credit in fear of economic liability or the overzealous persons accepting the normative obligation and consequentially overextending themselves?

Ironically, consumer credit (or owing money) was socially discouraged until the middle portion of the 20th century. The post–World War II era produced a spending boom fueled by readily available consumer credit. Owing money was no longer considered a social stigma.

Similarly, there is a process of status negotiation involved in this process. Consumer functions served as a positive economic link between the individual and economic institutional forces. The opening of these economic links transformed the conceptualization of the role of consumer credit. Consumer credit was an extension of our everyday lives rather than an outside intrusion on traditional social habits.

The continued extension of consumer credit inevitably increased numbers of people incapable of handling their finances. The economic sector can deal with those people by permanently stigmatizing them for aberrant social behavior. Consumer credit privileges are easily granted or withdrawn. The bankruptcy already appears on their credit files for seven to ten years.

Another option emerged as the number of bankruptcies increased over the last forty years. Bankruptcies were excused as a penalty for overemphatic participation within the economic sector. A previously negative connotation of individual failure was transformed into a "boys will be boys" mentality. Ironically, bankruptcy applicants are the most ideal recipients for new credit cards or other extended economic resources. These consumers cannot reapply for bankruptcy protection for another seven year period.

The industrial sector may have been too effective in its social control efforts. The ideal customer actively engages in consumer credit activity and makes regular payments. This economic pattern is one end of the process. A less desirable consequence develops when someone acquires the reputation for abusing these privileges and "going in over their head." Industrial concerns neutralized the objections concerning consumer debt as an undesirable practice. Cutting off consumer credit for enthusiastic customers endangers retail volume. Placing the delinquent individuals on a leash and permitting continued credit participation is a far more preferable option.

Institutions incorporated in the analysis include retail distribution networks and advertising agencies. These institutions are responsible for commissioning the production of consumer goods, ensuring the availability of these items, and marketing the advantages of the appropriate goods and services. The ongoing storyline pinpoints how these activities produced a historical change in consumer behavior. Consumer credit as an economic innovation offers some clues about how individual behavior is altered by outside social forces.

An analysis of statistical debt, along with information derived from interviews with executives placed in advertising, retail and credit card companies and banking circles will test this assertion.

RISE OF THE CONSUMER SECTOR

A social historical view of the consumer society indicates several important evolutionary changes. The capitalist process culminated in the establishment of an emphasis on consumer commodities. Automobiles and homes are two major examples of the impact that consumption (in the form of consumer wants or needs) has effected upon American society. The automobile is probably the most significant social invention of the twentieth century. People were afforded increased mobility for occupational, residential and recreational choices. Major corporations and factories subsequential relocated or were established in previously undeveloped areas, and an expansion in the tourist industry developed as a result of the ascendence of the automobile.

Mass production of the automobile did not occur until the early 1900s (Ewen, 1976). Originally, automobiles were particularly expensive and only the affluent could afford the newly accepted transportation alternative. Henry Ford sparked a consumer revolution with the production of the Model T. This marked the first time that automobiles (or other industrial products) were produced on an assembly line (Braverman, 1975). Workers built more automobiles than was heretofore possible. These machines were intended for consumer use. The rationalization was centered around an industrial sector belief that the public would buy the product.

Changes in the manufacturing system carried a dual impact in fulfilling this plan. In one respect, a market for this new product was necessary. Ford solved that problem by increasing workers' wages and shortening the work week. Ford also instituted an installment plan wherein workers could purchase the automobile through regular payments. Workers now had the capability of purchasing a product which they collectively mass produced (Harvey, 1989).

The development of home construction on a mass production level was another product of the consumer revolution. Rapid acceptance of the automobile enabled greater mobility in the exodus from major urban areas. Many items treasured by consumers, including homes, were previously given low priority. Families were reestablished with the culmination of the second world war and people were seeking previously unavailable consumer products. Rubber, metal and other materials were now available after being used during the war by the military industry for weapons production.

These items were now mass produced and spurred the post war affluence. Homes were built to accommodate the pent-up demand for consumer comfort. Veterans and others could obtain mortgages based upon low postwar rates (Polenberg, 1980). A mass construction of entire communities was planned and supervised by William Levitt. Subsequently called Levittown in honor of its founder, these communities stimulated growth of suburban areas. Consumer services spread beyond the previously settled urban areas. Shopping centers and some urban conveniences were established in these new locales.

RISE OF CONSUMER CREDIT AMIDST CAPITALIST DEVELOPMENT

The foregoing analysis was predicated upon the development of advanced capitalist societies. An advanced capitalist society was characterized by the exchange of surplus goods in a competitive marketplace. Necessary organization for achieving this goal produced bureaucracy as the cost of efficient exchange. An elaborate industrial apparatus predicated upon the dissemination and management of consumer credit information emphasized the maximization of profit and careful control of consumer selection.

Retailing or marketing organizations derived their social control potential through generational consumer dependence. The eventual legitimation of designated officials and their organizations assumed a substantial impact upon the consumer position. The organizational structure convinced consumers that accumulation represented an affirmation of acquired consumer social status. The impact emerged as consumers strived for accumulation through the acquisition of manufactured goods.

Economic success was linked with cultural recognition and symbolic capital. Acquisition of social status elevated the profile of industrial producers. The "captains of industry" during the latter portion of the nineteenth century and early part of the twentieth century were transformed into revered role models (Lowenthal, 1948). Lowenthal utilized content analysis in tracing the development of popular culture through documenting the idolization of conspicuous industrialists (e.g., Ford and Chrysler). He claims that the social focus was altered with the emphasis on active consumer behavior. New role models in the form of popular entertainers or sports stars gradually supplanted these industrial giants. Cultural expectations adapted in succeeding generations throughout the 20th century viewed consumer spending with increasing favor.

One cautionary note is necessary in the explication of these social historical trends. Bourdieu (1984), Bell (1976b) and other social critics realize that the Protestant Ethic was a reification of idealized expectations rather than an actual phenomenon.[19] Weber (1902) acknowledged that the emergence of organizational rationality downplayed the ultimate influence of asceticism and virtuous social sacrifice. The actual consumer culture accepts Weber's premise as developing more relevance during the post industrial and later postmodern (or post-Fordist) eras. This point is reemphasized by the contributions of Bell (1976a, 1976b), O'Connor (1982), and other commentators.

Convergence between Marxist and capitalist priorities emerge at this point in the analysis. Capitalists are concerned about the expected supply and demand, consumer consumption patterns and the transformation between wants and needs. Adherents of social system theory firmly support the legitimacy of the entrepreneurship mechanism.

The profit goals justified the means of altering consumer behavior through marketing and other enticements. Modern conveniences and attainment of ever emerging products were emphasized over traditional standards. The antiquated railroad flat depicted in the classic 1950s *Honey-*

mooners television series (starring Jackie Gleason) is supplanted with the advent of newly available technology within the next decade.

Marxists expand this notion into concern about the impact of these changes. The Marxist view places greater emphasis upon capitalist exploitation within the economic sphere and inequities built into the system. According to Marxists, the capitalist class acquired its considerable social economic control over several decades and facilitated redefined social expectations.

The overall analysis will not concentrate heavily upon the critical progression from central to market economy. Nevertheless, social control mechanisms essentially for supporting the market economy are built into the cultural system and remain a facet of the consumer credit revolution. Subsequent analysis will extend the Marxist perspective into the more "atheoretical" view that built-in specialization of a culturally based context drives the consumer oriented production of goods or experiences. Consumers purchase images as much as tangible or material goods.

The result supports the creation of a post-Fordist or niche marketing emphasis. The emphasis upon product or experiential diversification strengthens a constantly shifting cultural base offering more choices or experiences than in previous generations. Subsequent analysis leads through contextualized experiences, marketing, retail and the creation of mall culture, and a reconsideration of the social meaning associated with bankruptcy and consumer credit default.

NOTES

1. Personal choice is a reference to consumer products intended for fulfillment of leisure- or work-related fulfillment.

2. These distinctions were created by Ogilvy and Mather as part of a successful American Express Green Card advertising campaign. See the *New York Times* (1991).

3. See the remainder of this chapter and subsequent chapters on cultural shifts, advertising, retailing, and the social conception of bankruptcy.

4. These perspectives explain the role of consumer credit in American society, the individual motivations for using borrowed funds, and the larger significance of interest rate levels. Consumer orientation toward consumer debt has been analyzed by sociologists on several occasions, notably by Jay Bass (1977) and David Caplovitz (1965, 1974). Most analyses of consumer credit, starting with Bass, have dealt with consumer debt and the plight of the overburdened consumer (Bass, 1981). Bass was concerned with the social forces emphasizing consumer debt and the debt collection industry. Bass (1977) drew on a more extensive dissertation study in her analysis of the consumer credit industry and structure of the debt collection industry. Analysis developed in the present study draws upon Bass's previous research and specific conclusion regarding the consumer debt accumulation process.

Others, starting with Caplovitz, drew on social science interviews and survey data in an assessment of the retailing options available in ghetto neighborhoods and how people struggle with consumer debt. These analyses interpret consumer debt as an overall phenomenon affecting the general societal population. Caplovitz's research on consumer buying patterns and the consequences of debt is accorded further analysis in this study.

5. Post-Fordism refers to a social tendency toward diversified production and consumption of consumer goods and services. The name is derived from the standardized assembly-line procedures devised by Henry Ford in the early twentieth century. The consumer could have any car he or she wanted providing it was a Black Model T. David Harvey (1989) discusses the political economic transformation of late twentieth century capitalism and the transition from Fordism to flexible accumulation.

6. The overall experience of total social control of our working and leisure lives has been addressed by neo Marxists (Marcuse, 1964) and more current postmodern writers (see Baudrillard's [1983] study of Las Vegas). Juliet Schor (1991) offers an analysis of why leisure time is more constricted due to unnecessary work beyond the point of producing a profit. Schor's *The Overworked American*, offers the thesis that longer working hours exacerbate the work-and-spend cycle. Therefore, capitalist control over our everyday lives is enhanced as we work in order to spend and spend in justifying longer working hours.

7. I have visited Las Vegas, Disney World, Disneyland, Epcot Center, and the Fantasuite locations discussed in a later chapter. Many postmodern writers refrain from experiencing such attractions firsthand for fear of contaminating their own individual point of view. Contrast my impressions with those of Zukin (1991) and other writers within the popular postmodern genre.

8. The implication is that consumer capital in the form of purchased cultural experience takes precedence over labor-intensive processes during the Fordist assembly-line era. Henry Ford realized that tendency in the mass marketing of the Model T through installment credit extension.

9. See Ewen's (1976, 1988, Ewen and Ewen, 1982) intellectual trilogy highlighting the dependence upon image making and capitalist emphasis on niche marketing.

10. There is an extensive body of literature on privacy invasion via bureaucratized banking system operations. See Rule, McAdam, Stearns, and Uglow (1980); and Smith (1980).

11. Individuated products serving consumer choice and having cultural significance are introduced into the economic sector. These commodities transcend Henry Ford's dictum that consumers can purchase "any Model T as long as it is black."

12. Paranoia is used as a feeling that the capitalist society is instrumental in producing false consciousness or adverse individual frustration. This notion runs counter to the running theme of culture and symbolic tatus representation.

13. A forthcoming discussion of the credit card industry's development will bear out this analysis.

14. Background provided by Pierre Bourdieu's *Distinction: A Social Critique of the Judgment of Taste* (1984) and Fred Hirsch's *The Limits to Growth* (1976) will substantiate this categorical analysis.

15. The point of purchase refers to department store cashier stations. The chapter on retail operations details how electronic funds transfer systems (EFTs) and automated teller machines (ATMs) facilitate such purchases in department stores and supermarkets.

16. See the more detailed discussion of Foucault (1977) and socially created control mechanisms as presented in the next chapter of this book.

17. See analyses offered in the next chapter. Especially note the work of Bellah, Madsen, Sullivan, Swidler, and Tipton (1985) and Foucault (1977) as they point out that social character is pivotal in the derivation of individual choice. Consumer values, along with the culturally conditioned place of social status (Bourdieu, 1984), form a central thesis for the discussion offered in subsequent chapters.

18. The utopian planners insist that the market is always ripe for new products. Alvin Toffler in *Future Shock* (1973), addresses a changing corporate and consumer environment as an important factor in evolving consumer needs.

19. Intellectual speculation surrounds a controversy consisting of whether the Protestant ethic was always an ideological construction rather than a social reality. According to comments by Joseph Bensman in numerous classes on the sociology of Max Weber, the Protestant ethic was predominantly neutralized during the latter portion of the nineteenth century by the formation of a consumer culture.

2

Advent of Post-Fordist Cultural Developments

The previous chapter accounted for consumer activity as a form of affirmed social recognition.[1] Linkages between credit standing and overall status formulation (or reputation) were viewed as instrumental in encouraging the consumer revolution. Technical, historical and ideological components contributed toward bolstering consumerism as a way of life.

In sum, American society has moved from a focus on an information-driven technical or industrial workforce to an emphasis on the actual produced goods and their marketing potential. Developments connected with the bridge between the postindustrial economic system and the more recent post-Fordist cultural era form a vital portion of the offered analysis.

Consumer credit assumes a significant cultural economic role in transforming American society through the facilitation of commodity marketing and subsequent distribution. According to many experts, marketing is considered during the planning stages before the production of tangible goods.[2] Piore and Sable (1984) elaborate upon the concept of flexible specialization (otherwise termed niche marketing) in their analysis of the changing economic system.[3] Harvey (1989) offers a similar viewpoint in a discussion of flexible accumulation. New products are created for a preexisting or fabricated set of consumer desires. The diversified range of products and their predetermined or created consumer markets plug directly into the American cultural system.

Consumer credit, through advertising promotion or publicly acknowledged product utility, offers tourists and consumers a free rein on tapping into product or experience acquisition as cultural capital. Prestige and status, as much as utility, drive the development of the marketplace. Every object, whether a physical entity or an intangible experience, carries a particular value or personal meaning. Thus, a Disney World vacation assumes values stemming from an imputed value. The cultural appropriation (association between a tangible product or a manufactured environment) surrounding Disney World and other theme parks (along with assorted tourist attractions) gives these commodities a legitimated social status.

A brief history of consumer credit development from the early 1900s through the early 1990s incorporates an explanation of how current culture constantly evolves. Postindustrial society was dependent on stimulated consumer activity stemming from industrial effort. In effect, workers desired to exchange their wages for consumer goods and available cultural experience.

The distribution of the produced goods or new services was accomplished through a new middle-class professional group striving for upward mobility. New social classes were created with the democratization of consumer activity. The rise of the middle class in the period between 1890 and 1920 created the impetus for a postindustrial society (Smock, 1958; Bass, 1977; Bell, 1976b). The modernist formation of new lifestyle choices and status categories gives way to postmodern stress on flexibility and constant change.

The postindustrial society was formed through a combination of sociohistorical forces. Ewen (1976) characterized the socio-historical forces as conditions promoting marketing, consumer processes, and acculturation of the mass public with the temptation of consumer credit. The resultant postindustrial society, rife with its various cultural contradictions, emphasizes a pronounced information technology (Bell, 1976a).[4]

Information technology systems emphasized within a postindustrial society are an essential component of the cultural climate encouraging instant consumer gratification. Flexible accumulation is encouraged through the immediate dispensing of cash or transfer payments. Hendrickson (1974) documents how credit cards and information storage capacity can facilitate a cashless society through information transfer systems. Credit card-based technology enables the development of instant cash transfers through banking automatic teller machines, debit cards, or such programs as Master Teller. Such systems provide cash or instant fulfillment of everyday needs. Further accessibility to immediate cash, whether at a racetrack, department store, or neighborhood bank, enables the purchase of goods or services not immediately obtainable with credit cards.

An understanding of the information technology forces and cultural shifts discussed by Bourdieu (1984) and Harvey (1989) helps to build a framework explaining the transition from the postindustrial era to the postmodern era. This chapter incorporates these elements in the evolution from the Fordist era into the age of credit card utility for essential social services and discretionary consumer products.

MARKETING TANGIBLE GOODS AND CULTURAL EXPERIENCE

Marketing schemes developed following the postindustrial economic phase incorporated two important factors: (1) commodity distribution as a form of social control and (2) reinforcement of individual character structure. The economic system comports a semblance of control over consumer spending and the penalties for nonpayment of accumulated debts.

Foucault's objectives in *Discipline and Punish* (1977) are tangentially concerned with the analysis of marketing the conformative effects produced through consumer credit. The power to punish is an extension of the legal code and a result of effective economic control over societal institutions:

Punishment, then will tend to become the most hidden part of the penal process. This has several consequences: it leaves the domain of more or less everyday perception and enters that of abstract consciousness; its effectiveness is seen as resulting from its inevitability, not from its visible intensity; it is the certainty of being punished and not the horrifying spectacle of public punishment that must discourage crime; the exemplary mechanics of punishment changes its mechanisms. (p. 9)

Foucault's important analysis featured a historical analysis of the development and reformist tendencies within the prison system. Foucault pointed out that punishment incorporates significant social dimensions. His discussion of punishment provided a general utility beyond the simple punishment of an offender for the violation of perceived criminal offenses. According to Foucault, punishment becomes "the most hidden part of the penal process" (p.9). Punishment is characterized as an inevitable result of certain organizational calculation discouraging deviant activity.

Foucault continued his discussion of general deterrence with clarification surrounding why the state (or, in this case, organizational forces) must impose punishment. The state in this analysis can represent any institutions with cultural economic control. The effect of punishment is ritualized into a display of reality reaffirming the power of the dominant institutional force (p.57). The resultant reality subsequently undergoes reification following reinforcement and eventual public acceptance.

Foucault presented a further point about the social contract and the need for systematic punishment.[5] Societal control over everyday activities creates a common labeling of rule breakers as social enemies. An individual is subjected to the condition of punishment upon the violation of legal definitions. According to Foucault (1977): "Every malefactor, by attacking the social rights, becomes, by his crimes, a rebel and a traitor to his country; by violating its laws he ceases to be a member of it; he even makes war upon it" (p. 57).

Punishment is retributive within an applied generalizable social context utilizing Foucault's overall view. Consumer credit, along with its interlinks designating honorific status, is a signification of socio-economic acceptance or rejection. The credit reporting system provides a means of sanctioning consumers with questionable credit utilization patterns. Marketing criteria separate the most desirable from marginal credit risks. Commodity acquisition is blocked when consumer credit is never granted or after an established "negative" credit pattern.

An inherent contradiction exists in the above proposition. On the one hand, the success of niche marketing was predicated on the ideal that consumers required economic resources for the consumption of numerous emerging goods and services. The exclusion of a number of willing consumers circumvents the market demand for many culturally desirable products. The circumstances in this later stage of post-Fordist economic structure dictate extending consumer credit to both excellent and marginal credit risks. The punishment is a "hell" consisting of more consumer spending because the economic system cannot afford the loss of motivated consumer activity.

Bellah, Madsen, Sullivan, Swidler, and Tipton (1985) take this measure one step further. *Habits of the Heart* focuses on cultural control from within social institutions. The authors discuss everyday beliefs and the transformation of social class definitions through the intervention of social customs. According to Bellah's observations, economic structure is one element in a larger social system. Commitment is one element within a larger consideration of the closeness between social expectations imposed by society and individual choice.

Bellah et al. draw heavily from Reisman's (1950) scholarly contributions. Reisman (1950) offers a discussion of social adaptation in explaining the extension of commitment in everyday social life. The inner-directed person accepts the cultural expectation of acquiring material objects or rejecting the latest social appearances.[6]

Bellah et al. (1985) began with the derivative of their research perspective:

The fundamental question we posed, and that was repeatedly posed to us, was how to preserve or create a morally coherent life. But the kind of life we want depends on the kind of people we are—on our character. (p. vii)

Bellah et al. elaborated on this framework with a rationale for utilizing Tocqueville's (1830) vision of American life. The central problem for *Habits of the Heart* and a substantial subtheme for this study concerns De Tocqueville's conception of individualism.[7] De Tocqueville's emphasis on mores (termed "habits of the heart") focused on the nature of American character. Emphasis was placed on family life, religion, and political participation. De Tocqueville's only concern was whether individualism might isolate Americans from one another (Bellah et al., 1985, p. vii).

Bellah, et al. further define the central focus of their study of American character. They claim that individualism might destroy the forces that moderate the potential for democratic freedom. Further, they discuss the influence of culture, along with cultural traditions and practices, and how those traditions "limit and restrain the destructive side of individualism and provide alternative models for how Americans might live (p. vii).

Punishment and rugged individualism are two important elements instrumental in analyzing the impact of consumer credit. These elements were important considerations accounting for how consumer credit became a powerful cultural and economic force in American society. In *The Good Society*, a followup to their earlier work, Bellah, Madsen, Sullivan, Swidler, and Tipton (1991, pp. 210–211) analyze an intrinsic conflict present in most considerations of the shift from the religious to the secular-based cultural ideology guiding society. Culture and community clash as forces seeking to preserve traditional values through imposition of sanctions on consumer credit.

In a discussion of religion in the community, secularism and the search for individuality were attacked by Christian leaders. Bellah et al. claim that Christian theologists viewed consumerism as dangerous because "Consumerism kills the soul, as any good Augustinian can see, because it places things before the valuing of God and human community. It deadens our consciousness and thickens our senses" (pp. 210–211).

The perspectives of Bellah and colleagues (1985, 1991) are seemingly derivative of earlier research efforts. Reich (1970) argued that people reach their potential personal growth levels through cultural experience. Political and social barriers are restructured when individuals invest concerted effort in expanding their own capabilities. A prolonged attack on group values and stress on individualistic success often result from this selfishness.[8]

Although the passage of 20 years has disproved Reich's assertions on the growth of progressive ideas advanced in political movements, his points on the nature of social structure and community formation are still worth reiterating. Reich claims that a coming revolution will culminate with changes in the political structure:

There is a revolution coming. It will not be like revolutions of the past. It will originate with the individual and with culture. And it will change the political structure only as its final act. It will not require violence to succeed, and its impact cannot be successfully resisted by violence. It is not spreading with amazing rapidity, and already our laws, institutions, and social structure are changing in consequences: It promises a higher reason, a more human community, and a new and liberated individual. Its ultimate creation will be a new and endearing wholeness and beauty—a renewed relationship of man to himself, to other men, to society, to nature and to the land. (p. 4)

Reich continues in an extrapolation of how this change in our social climate will impact on everyday lifestyles. He refers to the material and cultural capital[9] that is consumed in the process of forming our everyday roles. Cultural changes have an impact on American consumers. Reich indicates how everyone is affected by this change:

It is a revolution of a new generation—a system typified by protest, rebellion, culture, clothes, music, drugs, rays of thoughts, liberated life styles are not a passing fad or form of dissent and refusal, nor in any sense irrational. Necessity and inequality will include youth and all people. (p. 4)

Reich's speculative notion of cultural revolution eventually evolved into social reality. Reich's speculations portended the rise of poststructural thought. Cultural values emphasize the utility of consumer credit as symbolic capital in acquiring social status. The inner-directed person from the 1960s and early 1970s was transformed into the young urban professional of the 1980s. Greed and self-aggrandizement were emphasized over sacrifice.

Reputations are built upon outward appearances and lifestyles rather than hard work. The "me generation" was typified by Michael Milken and other free-spending megamillionaire executives. The purported prosperity was a feature within the larger society. Average persons emulated the ultrarich through free spending on consumer credit accounts.[10] Consequences of the incredible spending sprees within the past decade are still reverberating in the debt-ridden 1990s.

Consequences of a free-spending society were foreseen in Reich's work. The relationship between consumer values, economy, and modern life was also discussed. Reich (1970) claimed that the economy was eversubject to the forces of inflation, occupational obsolescence, and the expense incurred while living in urban environments. The urban environment displaces nature with "expensive substitutes—television, instead of a Sunday ball game with local friends." Planned obsolescence is a major factor—the product becomes more complicated and existing products are replaced by new and improved models (p. 161).

Reich then offers a critique of capitalist society. The implied alienation associated with a transition from an industrial through a postindustrial and finally to a postmodern society is addressed in Reich's commentary on the process of substitution. He posits a claim that "continued growth depends upon creating new wants, developing new goods and services." The following quote best expresses Reich's ideas:

One cannot sell anything to a satisfied man. Ergo, make him want something new, or take away something that he has and then sell him something to take its place. Take away man's appreciation of natural body odors and then sell him deodorants and perfumes. Remove adventure from daily life and substitute manufactured adventure on television. Make it hard for an adult man to enjoy physical sport and give him a seat in a stadium to watch professional play. Give him less time to cook and sell him instant dinners. It has always been contended that the logic of commerce is improvement: make a better mousetrap and everyone will profit. But that is only what some optimists hope will be the result of commerce. The logic of commerce is simply to sell, whether the product is better or worse. (p. 162)

Reich is commenting that the logic of capitalism is bound in the manufacture of images and the shaping of everyday values. The creation of symbolic (or real) capital is a specific target of these changes (see Zukin, 1990). The developing poststructural (or post modern perspective) focuses on the relationship between economic structures and everyday consciousness as inherent in an everchanging economic climate.

BOURDIEU AND A CULTURE-BASED ANALYSIS OF CONSUMERISM

Bourdieu (1984)[11] argues that material acquisition is a class-based social pattern supported by anticipatory status attainment. Bourdieu examines the relationship between cultural expression and honorific community standing. Consumer goods acquired in the name of cultural expression are symbolic of status achievement assigned by general social consensus.

More important, Bourdieu is focusing on the reintegration between the economic and cultural dimensions of society. Class distinctions within the economy subsequently generate economic distinctions within the cultural realm. Both economic and cultural factors regenerate and legitimate the class structure. In effect, everyday cultural values are associated with a viable economic system supplying the basis for distinguishing particular social class segments. In other words, class and status are intricately related dimensions of social life.

Gartman (1991) posited several important observations in an important critique of Bourdieu's theoretical framework. Gartman observed that Bourdieu employs a "substantive Veblenesque concept of culture as a system of social symbols revealing relative position in a game of invidious distinctions" (p.422).[12]

Additionally, Gartman asserts that Bourdieu abandons the concept of people as cultural actors engaged in praxis and capable of revolutionizing and reproducing class systems. Instead, class structure is internalized within individuals and expressed as symbolic representations. The accompanying social class choices become symbolic standards dictating quality of life and social meaning as reflected by cultural representations. Cultural representations act as distinctions that social members utilize while engaged in reintegrating the realities of culture into social class standing.

Gartman's critique also includes another important point. Bourdieu considers the consumption of symbolic goods and the reproduction of class domination through legitimation and selection. Self-interests and economic behavior are related to economic realities and cultural practices. People pursue scarce goods and maximize profits in economic and cultural fields. In effect, the combination of both factors produces and sustains the continuing consumption dynamic in everyday life.

Gartman is correct in observing that Veblen (1899/1967) was noted for advancing this position in a discussion of invidious emulation.[13] Hirsch's (1976) principle of positional goods is another such example of status symbols established through economic and cultural control. Hirsch asserted that specific positional goods (or status-laden objects) are monopolized by upper-class societal members. Some examples of these goods include caviar, formal clothing ensembles, and antiques.

Gartman (1991) elaborates in noting that people in cultural contexts employ "capital" acquired or inherited in their efforts to maximize resources. These resources constitute cultural capital, also expressed as symbolic abilities, tastes, and goods. Ownership of these goods is regarded as "symbolic profits" derived for social honor or prestige. In effect, Bourdieu focuses on class conflict as a limiting force in the overall class structure. Gartman observes that Bourdieu's conception of class struggle is confined to the struggle for power between the "dominant and dominated factions of the bourgeoisie and the struggle for symbolic capital within the latter" (p.438). The interclass conflict "never fundamentally challenges the class struggle of capitalism, since all bourgeois factions have an interest in their joint domination of the working class" (p. 438).

Gartman aptly states that Bourdieu's interpretation of cultural change (as related to habitus or class position determining consumption) is not caused by fundamental struggles between classes with "inherently divergent interests" (p.439). Gartman places an emphasis on Bourdieu's analysis of "shifts in resources between individuals and class fractions maneuvering in cultural markets to monopolize symbolic capital" (p. 439). The dominated class of capitalism is almost completely passive and powerless. But cultural capital (or cultural practices and goods) ia desired by the working class because the "taste" is forced on them by their subordinate class position.

Bourdieu accepts the principle that the bourgeoisie acquires a taste for freedom, while the working class accepts a taste for necessity. Workers so thoroughly internalize their own domination that they inevitably rely on the symbolic tools created externally by bourgeois intellectuals. In effect, workers accept noncritical values defined by a dominant class.

The commercial analogy of workers desiring Grey Poupon mustard is one example where snob appeal is expressed as cultural capital filtering into lower- and middle-class consciousness. "The common person" desires symbolic or cultural commodities signifying distinctions conveyed through gaining possession of material or nonmaterial resources. The videocassette recorder, automobile, artwork, travel experience, and even the snobbish Grey Poupon mustard in current commercials are commodities purchasable by most social class groups. Niche marketing with products targeted for specific groups is also achieved in this fashion. Acquisition of more expensive items immediately unaffordable for some people is facilitated through the use of credit cards and installment credit plans.

CONSUMER CREDIT AND POST-FORDIST ECONOMIC DEVELOPMENT

An understanding of the postmodern era of cultural diversity and constant change facilitated by the availability of consumer credit must begin elsewhere. The credit card industry began in an earlier time. Details explaining the development of credit card utilization, attitudes toward credit card use, and the changing societal acceptance of credit cards are reflected within the shifts from industrial, postindustrial, post-Fordist, and post-modern eras.

Mandell (1990) documents the development of the credit card industry, aspects of economic growth within the credit card industry, the influence of technology, and current changes in the credit card industry. A consideration of these aspects must take into consideration the current level of credit card growth. Mandell reports that 1988 statistics on credit cards indicated that there were nearly 1.25 billion credit cards in circulation worldwide (p.xi). Consumers charged nearly $375 billion on their credit cards—12.6 percent of total consumer spending for all goods and services.[14]

The overall development of the credit card industry approximates the transition from the industrial to the postmodern economic phases. During the early twentieth century, acceptance of consumer credit took off with the demand for durable goods (automobiles, washing machines, vacuum cleaners, and other big ticket household goods). Credit cards were already issued by some US hotels, oil companies, and department stores. The earliest credit cards served to identify a customer with a charge account and provide merchants with a mechanism for keeping a record of customer purchases (p. xii).

Credit cards also constituted an extension of preexisting installment plans. Credit cards acted as a mechanism in forming allegiance between wealthy customers and a given store and generated sales of higher-priced items. Gasoline cards were issued in the 1920s as more consumers began buying automobiles. The growing airline industry started issuing installment credit in 1936 and would later establish a credit card operation. Later advances included minimum monthly payments, finance charges, and 30-day grace periods (p. xii).

The transition from the industrial to the post-industrial period was in full swing. The end of World War II spurred a strong consumer demand for durable products and economic means for affording vacation experiences. The US industrial base was engaged in mass production of consumer durables such as stoves, refrigerators, automobiles and other goods (pp. xiii-xiv).

Ehrenreich (1990; pp. 247–248) would say that this era was the beginning of the end for the middle-class. Consumer credit became a mainstay for establishing a middle-class existence throughout the transition of employment from the manufacturing sector into the service jobs associated with the postindustrial period. The period identified with "traditional values" would shift into a more modern epoch with the demand for diversified goods and services—the so called post-Fordist period. Niche marketing and diversification gave way to an image-enhanced lifestyle characterized by a greater demand for goods, services, and the accessing of available experiences (pp.247–248).

According to Ehrenreich, the demand for materialist products and the newly realized middle-class mobility went beyond the surface improvements in living conditions (p.248). Emotional and structural consequences resulted from the economic transition:

The clamor for tradition is not, as many seem to think, part of an overdue pendular swing away from the hollow modernism of disposable loyalties, short attention spans, and easy comforts. "Traditional values" are merely a counterpoint to modernism, perhaps an inevitable feature of it. The broader the path to what appears to be laxity and surrender, the louder the calls for discipline and struggle. For the "new class" is not, as the intellectuals of the right have liked to think the locus or agent of hedonism. It is the locus of the most acute conflict over hedonism, the nexus of the most pronounced tension between modernism and tradition, consumerism and self discipline. (p. 248)

The "new class" accepted the new consumer values accompanying new professional status and economic means for affording the cultural signs of success in the broadened economic system. There is an interesting progression of thought on the significance of cultural success. The late nineteenth century and the early twentieth century was a time of transition from emphasis upon industry to a focus on consumers. Veblen (1899/1983) analyzed the spread of consumer values with a discussion of conspicuous consumption and invidious emulation. The upper classes and aspiring middle class sought to distinguish themselves from the emergent immigrant groups.

Hirsch (1976) contributed to the discussion with his claim that there are specific positional goods reserved for members of the upper echelon. Members of the middle class are left with the average-priced durables, while the lower classes aim for what is somewhat affordable.

Potter (1954) completes the analysis with a view of the lower-class aspiration to the materialist possessions enjoyed by the upper and middle classes:

In a society of consumption, as the Goodmans visualize it, production is only a means to the end of consumption, and therefore satisfaction in the work disappears. The workman accordingly focuses all his demand upon suitable working conditions, short hours, and high wages, so that he may hasten away with sufficient time, wealth, and energy to seek the goals of the consumer. This quest can be carried on only in a great city. And the chief drive toward such goods is not individual but social. It is imitation and emulation which result in the lively demand. At first, perhaps, it is "mass comforts" which satisfy cityfolk—these belong to the imitation of each other; but in the end it is luxuries; for these belong to emulation, to what Veblen used to call the "imputation of superiority." (p. 175)

The development of the credit card industry incorporated the basic change from an industrial-based economy into a more post-Fordist driven society. Harvey (1989) goes beyond the post-Fordist era in examining the roots of an eventual postmodern or poststructural society:

Most postmodern thinkers are fascinated by the new possibilities for information and knowledge production, analysis, and transfer. Lyotard (1984), for example, firmly locates his arguments in the context of new technologies of communication and, drawing upon Bell's and Touraine's theses of the passage to a "postindustrial information based society" situates the rise of postmodern thought in the heart of what he sees as a dramatic social and political transition in the languages of communication in advanced capitalist societies. (p. 49)

The postmodern perspective develops during a period of late capitalism. The images conveyed by an information-based society permit the transfer of knowledge from one place to another. Information on credit standing, and the issuance of credit card credit lines, is crucial as a form of cultural capital.

Credit cards, and the privileges attributed to possessing spending power, are vital social elements defining our position in society. Foucault (1977) would claim that we are victims of the information prison. He might rightfully believe that we are shaped and defined by contradictory cultural definitions of cultural success and measured by available economic resources.

THE RISE OF CONSUMER CREDIT

Bourdieu's framework (1984) provides a powerful understanding of how consumer credit evolved into a significant socio-economic force. The acquisition of products based on perceived individual taste is a strong motivating force in consumer acceptance of credit cards and installment debt.[15]

Credit cards and other forms of consumer credit made a slow evolutionary impact on American culture and political economic change. The material in this section traces the consumer credit industry from its infancy through its maturation in the 1970s and then its transformation into the information-processing capabilities of the post-Fordist era.

The history of credit card use corresponds with the full-fledged development of postindustrial society and the transition into the more recent postmodern system emphasizing cultural transformation. Niche marketing and the acceptance of flexible specialization provide the rationale for an ever expanding economic base.[16]

Credit allocation and diversified incentives or credit card premiums are factors stemming from the increasing industrialization of the American business sector. Credit cards facilitated the rise of consumer spending for consumer products or services. The democratized spread of credit card utilization originally began with a product marketed for the very affluent. The diversification of credit card allocation facilitates the spending ability of larger consumer populations and a pronounced trend toward niche marketing.

Additionally, extended services or other incentives associated with various credit card programs promote extended consumer choices. A sizable consumer market creates a competitive atmosphere. Financial institutions and industrial firms maximize market share through the creation of new services distinguishing one credit card from another. Rebates, credit toward industrial products, and specific premiums are aimed at enticing a greater share of the consumer credit card business.

The introduction of credit card circulation corresponds with the increase in postindustrial development. In the beginning, open-book payments were the preferred method of handling consumer credit. Consumers merely settled their bills with local merchants. However, merchants were continually concerned with identifying wealthy or steady customers and keeping records of customer payments. The credit card, as devised in 1914 for payment on retail purchases and in 1936 for airline travel, facilitated identification and enabled wealthy customers to pay according to a convenient onetime schedule. The trend toward merchant and consumer acceptance of credit cards is striking: According to Department of Commerce data, during the first half of 1930 only 47.4 percent of department store sales were made in cash; 7 percent were made on an installment contract basis, and the remaining 45.6 percent were open book (Mandell, 1990, p. 17).

Credit card use began to grow with the advent of industrialization and the early rise of the middle class during the 1930s. A small number of issuers among hotels, oil companies, and department stores initially served to distinguish the wealthy from the working class. But credit card issuance gradually increased until the mid-1930s. Credit cards served to generate business from customers who did not possess ready cash. In fact, Mandell (1990, p.18) points out that two thirds of Americans using credit cards by the mid-1930s did so because of harsh economic times. Remember that credit cards were still issued to select populations: businesspeople, automobile owners, and generally affluent citizens.

The postindustrial era enveloped American society after World War II. Americans now possessed discretionary income with the establishment of government programs guaranteeing pensions, worker's compensation, unemployment, and disability. Consumer credit stood at $5.7 billion in 1945. By 1970, it had grown to $143.1 billion, and by 1980 to over $375 billion, excluding mortgage debt (Mandell, 1990, p.17).

Diversification—or niche marketing—was more prosperous than at any time in our nation's history. The availability of durable goods, automobiles, and the establishment of theme parks or vacation areas (Las Vegas, Disneyland) in the period following World War II spurred on the consumer credit industry. Revolving charges were adopted by department stores such as Gimbel's, Bloomingdale's, Filenes, and Bambergers during the period from 1930 to 1950. We were moving away from a credit card industry dependent on sole management by individual vendors. A number of merchants—mainly large retail stores—banded together to form a cooperative card operation (Mandell, 1990, pp. 24–25).

Universal cards (all-purpose credit cards usable for obtaining diversified merchandise) became popular early in the 1950s. The universal cards allowed customer activity in many different business settings. Diners' Club proved that such a plan was profitable. The Diners' Club operation expanded into Europe during the mid-1950s with the proven ability to generate a profit. The Diners' club base consisted of merchants in industries such as hotels, airlines, gas stations, retail stores, and automobile rental companies.

Post-Fordist differentiation even impacted on the credit card industry. Merchant resistance to paying established discount fees led to the establishment of separate universal credit card categories—travel and entertainment (T&E) (American Express, Diners' Club, and Carte Blanche) and the bank cards (Bankamericard and Mastercharge). Each credit card found an individual niche market in accommodating the wealthy with more discretionary spending power (the T&E cards catered to the more affluent business class) or the average middle-class consumer (those individuals with a moderate income and some discretionary funds).

Ironically, each of the T&E or bank credit cards was established in response to competition from competing business interests. The post-Fordist influence is reflected in the 1958 entrance of American Express into the credit card business. American Express was worried that Diners' Club would impact substantially upon the international business traveler market. Carte Blanche was originally the private credit card of the Hilton Hotel Corporation. Formerly owned by First National City Bank, the credit card is now owned by the Avco Corporation (Mandell, 1990, p.29).

Banking institutions also envisioned credit cards as a product with the potential for creating enormous profit. The first bank credit card was issued by the Franklin National Bank in 1951.[17] By 1955, there were more than 100 banks with credit card plans. Larger banks still did not enter into the credit card field. Many banks introduced a new credit card plan during 1958–1959. The plan called for the option of repaying balances on a revolving credit basis. The Chase Manhattan Charge Plan was introduced in 1958, at the same time as BankAmericard initiated operation on the West Coast. Chase Manhattan had 350,000 cardholders and 5,300 retail merchants by the end of its first year of operation. However, the Chase plan collapsed in January 1962 when credit losses and operating expenses mounted (Mandell, 1990, p.29).

The collapse of the Chase credit card, along with the slow growth of the Bank of America card, slowed credit card industry growth. The credit card again became a viable product when the Bank of America started growing during the mid 1960s. In 1966, the Bank of America licensed the operation of the BankAmericard across the United States.

Several other major banks formed a competitive second national card system, which became known as the Interbank Card Association. Local cards became national cards serving a mobile American population with the desire for purchasing durable goods or just financing vacation travel. In 1969, the Interbank Card Association purchased the rights to "Mastercharge" from the Western States Bank Card Association. Now both major associations had a recognizable name, image, and trademark that they could market as a viable product. Both operations eventually evolved into completely independent industry groups (Mandell, 1990, p. 31).

The 1970s was a period responsible for setting up the economic boom during the following decade. The "me generation," actualized through credit card utilization, was transformed into a debt carrying "greed generation" wanting and buying everything in sight. A bellwether event signifying the 1980s generation impact occurred in 1980. President Jimmy Carter's fiscal policy measures intended for the control of inflation curtailed credit card issuance. The crisis quickly passed, with credit card companies repositioning themselves through television commercials telling customers that prudent purchasing was not pernicious. The same theme has occurred occasionally throughout the last two decades.

Consumer credit, particularly credit cards, was responsible for the important transition from actualizing the inner self to marching toward conspicuous consumption. Credit cards constituted an individual product that not only enabled access to durable goods or travel but also constructed an attributed image. The postmodern era of images dominating social discourse led to enhanced individual identity through the creation of new markets for emerging products. The emerging niche markets in the late capitalist search for profit broadened middle-class lives and strengthened the economic viability of a once-struggling credit card industry.

Each credit card became an individual commodity subsequently marketed as painstakingly as the facilitated purchases of consumer products or experiences. MasterCharge (which later became Mastercard), BankAmericard (which later became Visa), and American Express established a target consumer group and particular image. The Mastercard image was always the average consumer and family living; Visa concentrated on travel and self-actualization; and American Express was usually oriented toward the business traveler.

Greed was the watchword for the consumers spending over their economic means and the industry itself. Banks ensured eventual profit through a variety of different means. Financial institutions originally depended on installment charges for the realization of credit card profitability. However, they could not raise the interest rate above 18 percent per year.[18] They attempted implementing an average daily balance method for computing installment charges. Additionally, banks marketed other products to their customers ("cross-selling").[19] Marketing credit card utility through the post-Fordist packaging of other services was very successful. Early efforts in 1973 included the establishment of a Wells Fargo Gold Account program where a $36 fee gave the customer a check cashing identification card, unlimited free checking, free personalized checks, a safe deposit box, free traveler's checks, cashier's checks, money orders, a MasterCharge card, overdraft protection (using the credit line on the MasterCharge card), and reduced interest rates on personal loans (Mandell, 1990, p. 73).

Several major events contributed to the tremendous growth of credit cards during the 1980s. The post-Fordist tendencies within the credit card industry were most visible during the decade. Specific developments include the redefinition of credit cards as profit-generating instruments (or "cash cows" in financial terms), further differentiation among credit cards, the evolution of affinity cards, the creation of incentives differentiating specific credit cards, and the creation of industrial-based credit card programs.

The imposition of fees, establishment of credit cards issued by non bank organizations, and newly offered incentives transformed the credit card into a product with many disparate purposes. First, banks began charging annual fees for credit card ownership. American Express, Carte Blanche, and Diners' Club were the only credit card companies previously charging annual fees. They justified the extra cost because the card was marketed to successful corporate executives able to afford the costs and deduct such expenses as business fees.

The imposition of annual fees came at the same time as a dramatic drop in interest rates during the 1980s. Credit card interest rates remained at approximately 18 to 21 percent, while the cost of borrowing money from the Federal Reserve dropped below 10 percent. The annual fees ($20 for most Mastercards and Visas issued by banking institutions) and the high interest rates produced major profits for a previously marginal financial product. As a result, bank card operations began outperforming all other forms of bank debt.

Mandell (1990) points out that since 1984 bank credit card pretax margins exceeded those collected on real estate, installment, and commercial debt. This observation is documented with data showing that from 1984 to 1986 credit card returns averaged 3.6 percent, while the returns on other forms of bank debt were 2.4 percent on mortgages, 2.7 percent on consumer installment debt, and 1.4 percent on commercial and other loans (p. 78).

"GOING FOR THE GOLD"

Consumer debt was more prominent during the financially explosive 1980s decade. As noted by Mandell (1990), a study by Glenn Canner on the credit card industry from 1970 to 1986 revealed that the average outstanding balance more than doubled (from $649 in 1970 to $1,472 in 1986), even though the proportion of credit card owners using the revolving credit feature remained constant at 50 percent (p. 79).

Many banks recognized these factors. In fact, banks that previously rejected the efficacy of a credit card program accepted and heavily promoted the product. In 1979, only 71 percent of banks offered Mastercard or Visa. By 1985, 90 percent of all banks offered a Visa card and 87 percent a Mastercard. Mandell also offers the information that by the end of 1986, banks held nearly two thirds of total credit card outstanding balances, up from one half in 1982. Interestingly, credit card receivables had become 5 percent of total bank loans by 1986, up from 3 percent in 1982 (p. 79).

The financial and consumer image of the card was redefined in the period from 1986 to 1992. Credit cards were transformed from postFordist (or differentiated) products into a more postmodern image-driven financial instrument. Industry competition resulted in a reinvention of the credit card image. In a significant development, financial institutions began encroaching upon the American Express Company control of the prestige card market. The Mastercard Gold card was introduced in June 1981, and the Visa Premiere Card (later renamed Visa Gold) was marketed in 1982. The major competitors were American Express, along with Carte Blanche and Diners' Club (then owned by Citibank).

According to Mandell (1990), Visa Gold and Mastercard made major inroads in the market with a lower annual fee (under $40—slightly less than the $45 charged by the American Express green card and significantly less than the $65 charged for the gold card). The American Express green card was the most widely held and used prestige card in 1988. It accounted for more than 40 percent of the US market share in cards and 41.4 percent in volume followed by Mastercard Gold, Amex Gold, Diners' Club, and Carte Blanche. By 1988, Visa Gold and Mastercard Gold accounted for more than 37 percent of the prestige card market and more than 13 million cardholders. The Nilson Report predicted that the market share would reach 54 percent by 1990 and 69 percent by 1995 (p. 82). As Mandell aptly notes that the bank cards were accepted at 2.5 million merchant locations in the United States and at 5.9 million worldwide, as opposed to 1.4 million locations for American Express in the United States and 2.1 million worldwide (p. 87).

In retaliation, American Express reinvented the standard bank credit card with the introduction of the Optima Card in 1987. The Optima Card was a revolving credit card. By mid 1988, American Express had distributed 1.5 million Optima Cards and produced over $1 billion in revolving balances. The advantages of the $15 fee included acceptance at locations accepting the American Express card and a low variable interest rate (Mandell, 1990, p.83).

Interestingly, the marketing and counter-marketing strategies between the bank cards and the more prestigious travel and entertainment cards set the stage for introduction of the Discover Card and many competing third parties. The introduction of the Discover Card by Sears, Roebuck and Co. in 1986 significantly transformed the public image of the credit card. For the first time during the 1980s, a credit card was marketed as a "consumer friendly" financial instrument. The credit card did not include an annual fee and offered a rebate to users based on volume of purchases. Sears thought that the benefits were offsettable with a 19.8 percent interest rate (Mandell, 1990, p. 84).

Sears' introduction of the Discover Card triggered a redefinition of the credit card. Although the Discover Card was not originally profitable and still holds only 7.9 percent of the credit card market, consumers began demanding more in a credit card instrument.

The increasingly popular gold cards issued by banking firms eventually transformed all universal credit cards into postmodern marketing devices. The newly emerged gold credit cards took a page from Sears marketing strategy. The Gold Mastercard and the Visa Gold cards gave the consumer an extra "bang for the buck." The market was well saturated with credit cards by the mid 1980s. In an effort to compete with American Express, the bank gold cards offered the same consumer benefits. Buyer protection plans, wherein American Express replaced damaged products purchased on the American Express card, "lemon" protection offering protection from irreparable merchandise, and extended warrantee plans were now offered by the newly issued bank gold cards.[20]

The quest for profits through rebates and gold card–type benefits did not stop with the competition between the bankcard associations and the American Express Company. The issuance of affinity cards, gold card benefits on regular bank credit cards, and industrial-based credit cards changed the standard image of a credit card as a facilitator of enhanced purchasing power.

The credit card market reached a saturation point during the mid 1980s (Mandell, 1990). Most consumers already carried an average of three cards (bank and travel and entertainment). The number does not include department store cards or ATM cards. The competitive market for new customers necessitated new marketing strategies to persuade customers to change or add cards (p. 80).

Affinity card programs (wherein organizations sponsored various Mastercard and Visa marketing programs) began appearing in 1985. The new affinity cards assumed an individual identity. In contrast to traditional credit cards featuring the name of the bank across the top, the new affinity cards featured the names of organizations. The organization received 2 percent of the annual fees, purchases, or installment fees paid by the consumer.[21] By 1986, there were 296 affinity programs. According to Mandell (1990), affinity cards in circulation in 1988 numbered an estimated 26 million cardholders carrying 2,725 different cards with each bearing its own appearance (or image) (p. 80).

Affinity cards were successful for two reasons (Mandell, 1990). The personalized credit cards provided an incentive for the consumer to accept a new card or to switch from a previous card. According to a Visa study in 1988, affinity card solicitations produced two to three times the applications for cards as did solicitations for regular cards (p. 80). Additionally, targeting groups with known financial attributes resulted in reduced credit risk and often increased credit card spending volume. Mandell mentions that Citibank's frequent flyer program, in affiliation with American Airlines, has 200,000 cardholders whose average income is $75,000. On average, these credit cardholders ostensibly use their cards 14 times each month, whereas the average cardholder uses his or her card only 11 times per month. Additionally, a study cited in the November 11, 1988 issue of *Advertising Age* reported that 45 percent of consumers holding both affinity and traditional credit cards use the affinity card more often (p. 80). A Visa study also indicated that affinity cardholders spend more on their cards, and 44 percent said that the affinity card is the first Visa card that they have held (pp. 80–81).

Every special interest group jumped into the market (p. 80)—for example, the First Interstate Bank of California's Visa card for North American sheep supporters and the card promoted jointly by Breyer's Ice Cream and Marine Midland Bank. Mandell divides the affinity cards into three categories: product benefit cards, lifestyle cards, and personality cards (p. 80). The product benefit cards provide the cardholder with a specific benefit, such as frequent-flyer bonus miles for every dollar spent. Lifestyle cards are sponsored by particular groups, such as charitable causes. Mandell mentions a card issued by Commercial Federal in Omaha benefiting local Catholic schools and one issued by the Empire of America Federal Saving Banks benefiting AIDS (acquired immunodeficiency syndrome) research. Many cards distributed by charitable organizations benefit the organizations through donations from banks upon the success of the card programs. Personality cards focus on particular personalities such as the Elvis Presley card marketed by Leader Federal Bank for Saving in Memphis or the New York Giants card issued by First Fidelity Bank in Newark, New Jersey.[22]

Each credit card issuer now strives to create a product with a distinctive market image. There is nothing new in carving out a segment of the niche market for success in a competitive environment. The postmodern credit card was a product whose time had come. The issuance of the AT&T Universal Calling Card and industrial-based credit cards hastened the process. Spurred on by the limited success of the Discover Card and the widespread public acceptance of numerous affinity cards, AT&T and several industrial corporations entered the competitive credit card industry. AT&T, not unlike MCI and US Sprint issued its own calling cards. The advent of affinity cards led to introduction of a 1989 deal where Visa entered into an agreement with MCI Communications. The credit card enabled customers to make telephone calls and charge the calls on a general credit card. But the newer AT&T Universal Card was basically a general-purpose credit card. Anyone charging more than $10 per year could avoid paying an annual fee.

Post-Fordist and the more interesting postmodern reshaping of product image continued as a constant process. The concept of no annual fees and consumer rebates caught on in a saturated credit card field. The industry was clearly reconceptualizing the credit card as a viable product in a competitive industry. General Motors, followed by General Electric and Ford Motor Company, entered the credit card wars in 1992. The automobile industry needed a strong marketing product to stimulate the sale of new cars during a recessionary period. General Motors (GM) created an affinity MasterCard product that offered the consumer several advantages. First, the card was available to virtually anyone. Second, no fee was imposed for possession of the credit card. Lastly, 5 percent of the purchase volume up to $10,000 in goods and services annually on each card was applied to a downpayment on a new or leased General Motors car. Thus, not only was the consumer using a Mastercard in a normal purchasing manner; the economic image of accumulating a rebate applicable to a new car was equally enticing.

Materials accompanying issuance of the card define how the GM card rebate works. According to an advertising brochure, the GM card rebate automatically credits a consumer with a 5 percent cash rebate. Consumers are afforded the opportunity to accumulate up to $500 per year, up to a maximum of $3,500 over a period of seven years. The accumulated credits are applicable toward the purchase of a GM car or truck. Consumers are also given an option of applying the rebate to the downpayment.

GM also engages in cooperative marketing with other travel-related or entertainment concerns. According to accompanying material in the same mailing, using the GM Mastercard for charging telephone calls on the credit card, renting a card through Avis, staying at a Marriott Hotel, or purchasing magazines earns the same rebate package. The consumer earns a 5 percent rebate on every dollar spent on long-distance service charges. The rebate is doubled to 10 percent if the charges are actually billed on the GM card.

General Electric Company (GE) and Ford Motor Company entered the affinity Mastercard fray shortly thereafter. The Ford Motor Company combined with Citibank in enacting the same program as General Motors. General Electric, an industrial company marketing appliances instead of automobiles, proposed the same no annual fee/rebate deal as General Motors. Before the demise of the General Electric affinity card program in 1996, the difference was that General Electric's rebate applied to merchandise available in a catalog. Additionally, the GE card carried a $25 yearly fee, but there was no cap on the rebate program. The GE card clearly presented the same corporate benefits as the GM card. General Electric promoted a consumer loyalty based upon an incentive for using its credit card instead of a regular bankcard.

An analyst can argue that these programs are not totally different from the marketing efforts previously initiated by Mastercard and Visa. Consumers always accumulated Citidollars (or similar units) applicable toward purchasing merchandise available in a catalog. According to a representative from Chase Manhattan Bank, the long-standing rebate program offers merchandise as an incentive for using the card. The card is actually marketed as the product, not the eventual merchandise that the consumer can obtain through cardholder loyalty.

The newer rebate programs, along with the credit cards permitting accumulated frequent-flyer milage for phone call volume on MCI or US Sprint-sponsored Mastercard or Visa cards, are clearly significant. The consumer is rewarded for using a particular credit card. The merchandise is used as an enticement for continued credit card use. In effect, the credit card has been reinvented for the purpose of encouraging competitive market volume and product identification in an already saturated industry.

CONCLUSIONS

The credit card field reflects the distinct shift toward post-Fordist differentiation with an emphasis on marketing image. Various bank credit cards have virtually reinvented their consumer images in an attempt to grab an important segment of a growing niche market. Credit cards are not the only product sold as a consumer-friendly vehicle. Credit cards enable or facilitate the consumer acquisition of goods, services, and ultimately experiences.

Consumer credit, according to Foucault, Bellah, et al., Harvey, Bourdieu, and others discussed in this section, constitute a reward for believing in the social economic system. The acquisition of material status (or habitus) and economic success through individual striving and hard work encourages the development of a cohesive economic system built on everyday consumer values. Subsequent chapters examine how status formation and the transition from postFordist to postmodern status identification are operative in forces unleashed by the advertising industry, retail sector, and damage control when Foucault's image of socially exacted punishment is applied toward redefining bankruptcy as a social status.

NOTES

1. Consumer credit is a form of status recognition. In effect, people are seen as an extension of the symbolic or real capital possessed through everyday acquisition (Bourdieu, 1984). Marcuse (1964) expressed the same concept while claiming that community accumulation was a reflection of developing close identification with durable goods. The overall commodity accumulation process acted as an affirmation of social achievement.

2. Influential social thinkers from both perspectives include the following authors: postindustrial: Bell, 1976a, and Touraine, 1971; postmodern (or post-Fordist) Harvey, 1989, and Zukin, 1991. Articles derived from the postmodern tradition include Mike Featherstone's "Perspectives on Consumer Culture" (1990), and Sharon Zukin's "Socio-Spatial Prototypes of a New Organization of Consumption: The Role of Real Cultural Capital" (1990). In addition, the marketing perspective, as viewed from a postmodern framework, was incisively developed by William Leiss's *Limits to Social Growth*, (1978). An extension of the various perspectives developed by Leiss and other economic critics is offered elsewhere in this book.

3. Flexible specialization, or niche marketing, was considered in Piore and Sable's study of the implied changes following the postindustrial economic phase.

4. The real question is how this information is transferred into a commodity useful in planning and marketing. Touraine's (1971) discussion of a programmed society was especially meaningful within the parameters of a poststructural economic system dependent on careful marketing of the ATM and the cashless society.

5. Foucault (1977) admittedly states that the analysis of punishment draws on Durkheim's discussion of collective conscious.

6. See David Reisman's seminal discussion of social adaptation in *The Lonely Crowd* (1957).

7. Bellah, et al. (1985:324) define individualism in the following manner:

Individualism: A word used in numerous, sometimes contradictory, senses. We use it mainly in two: (1) a belief in the inherent dignity and, indeed, sacredness of the human person. In this sense, individualism is part of all four of the American traditions we have described in this book—biblical, republican, utilitarian individualist, and expressive individualist; (2) *a belief that the individual has a primary reality ontological individualism.*

This view is shared by utilitarian and expressive individualists. It is opposed to the view that society is as real as individuals, a view we call social realism, which is common to the biblical and republican traditions.

8. Reich intuitively foretold the coming of a politically correct movement on college campuses. The discussion of moral character and a higher moral plane emerged as justification for denouncing divergent social values.

9. Cultural capital and symbolic capital are compatible terms connoting an idealized quantification (or value) of our everyday activities and basic information technology. For example, a tourist experience at Disney World or Las Vegas has personal value tapping into cultural expectations created by the symbols within the immediate environment (i.e., specific cartoon characters or symbolism within the Las Vegas strip neon signs, architecture; or structured casino gaming procedures).

10. Consumer credit marketing was too effective. The "lifestyles of the rich and famous" during the 1980s were transformed into the "lifestyles of the downwardly mobile and debtridden." This theme attracted substantial media interest at a presentation co-organized by Lloyd Klein and Eva Bronstein-Greenwald at the 1985 annual meeting of the American Sociological Association (see Klein and Bronstein-Greenwald, 1985).

11. Bourdieu's *Distinction. A Social Critique of the Judgment of Taste*, Harvard University Press, 1984 was the culmination of several studies on consumer culture and social status.

12. Bourdieu (1984) also presents a reconceptualization of grand theory through the integration of Marx's (1860/1967) conception of bourgeois, petty bourgeois, and proletariat class categories and a linkage between Weber's (1946) influential concepts of class and status. In effect, we are again seeing "old wine in new bottles."

13. Veblen developed this perspective in *Theory of the Leisure Class* (1899/1967). Subsequent social thinkers pursued this line of inquiry in analysis of invidious emulation. For example, see Bensman (1976) and Hirsch (1975).

14. Mandell (1990) elaborated on the implications of the credit card revolution:

Armed with billions of credit cards, shoppers, business people, and travelers of all economic and social backgrounds from around the world now charge everything from vacations and business trips to groceries and hair dryers. Whether we call them bank cards, gas cards, retail cards, travel and entertainment cards, or simply the more familiar "plastic," there is little doubt that the credit card has revolutionized the marketplace. These thin, wallet-sized, plastic rectangles with their unobtrusively sophisticated magnetic strips are the keys that unlock the electronic vaults of banks, automated teller machines (ATMs), and cash dispensers around the world. They have become an essential element of daily life. With a credit card, you can buy yourself a new car. Without it, you cannot even rent one. (p. 25)

15. Many sociologists would claim that this is a vestige stemming from the reification of consumer values.

16. Flexible specialization is a concept describing the manufacture or provision of products and services intended for a diversified consumer population. See Piore and Sable (1984) for an extended discussion of changing economic capabilities and a consideration of expanding manufacturing capacity.

17. I have personally seen one of the original paper credit cards. During a 1983 research interview at American Express regarding bank security and credit card

fraud, I spoke with James Webb, a pioneer in the credit card industry since his employment at Franklin National Bank and then head of security at American Express. Webb pulled out his "goodie box" and showed me some of the early credit card instruments. The original Discover Card commercials featured a prototype embossed with the name "James L. Webb" was clearly a tribute to an innovator in the credit card business.

18. Citibank did get around that problem through moving its operations from New York to South Dakota, where the maximum usury rate was 21 percent.

19. Cross selling is still highly successful. Major banks bundle their credit cards with life insurance plans, travel clubs, dining and entertainment plans, dental plans, and legal services. American Express often sends out an overstuffed envelope containing available merchandise. Amoco also actively markets merchandise available through mail order and billable on the Amoco Card.

20. Information obtained from American Express marketing brochures (1986–1992).

21. The percentage of consumer purchases paid to the sponsoring organizations ensures a constant flow of capital for continued operation. Affinity cards issued by the Automobile Association of America (AAA) and the American Sociological Association (ASA) are two examples of such affinity cards.

22. Many sports teams sponsor affinity cards. The cardholder can earn points applicable toward gift merchandise and presumably benefit community organizations when the accumulated fees given to the sports teams are donated to specific charities.

3

Consumer Credit and the Experiential Realm

An analysis of consumer credit can assume a multidimensional perspective. The everyday conception of consumer credit extends beyond everyday credit card ownership and use as a financial device enabling the purchase of tangible consumer goods. Credit cards form the gateway for accessing experiences previously unaffordable to the average consumer. In effect, consumer credit also promotes and facilitates the acquisition of recreational activities, tourism, and the search for alternative social experiences.

Analysis offered in the upcoming discussion of leisure and tourism assumes that a social relationship exists between consumer culture and the consumption of tangible goods and intangible experiences (otherwise known as cultural capital). Credit card utilization facilitates leisure and the acquisition of cultural capital through arranging expensive airline travel, car rental, the attainment of food, lodging, souvenirs, and specialized tours, and providing cash for unexpected emergencies. Further, the images and experiences offered in the travel experience encompass a staged authenticity transferring sightseeing into a cultural pursuit. Workers can more easily achieve desired cultural experiences through utilizing their credit cards during the vacation or leisure activity.

This point is important for understanding an evolving emphasis on consumer activities and everyday social experience. We can start with Featherstone's (1991) notion that a normal sociological conception links consumer culture with the acquisition of manufactured goods (or the products stemming from the concept of the production of consumer items). According to Featherstone, these goods carry a specific exchange value justifying their pricing in the marketplace (p.14). The resultant exchange value is achieved with the relinquishing of workers' wages for the desired goods.

Marx (1860/1967) and members of the subsequent Neo-Marxist Frankfurt School (Horkheimer and Adorno, 1972; Marcuse, 1964; Lefebvre, 1971) reiterate the establishment of culture value inherent in the creation of markets for new commodities. According to Featherstone (1991), Marxists may claim that material acquisitions (consumer goods) produce enhanced opportunities for "controlled and manipulated consumption":

If from the perspectives of classical economics the object of all production is consumption, with individuals maximizing their satisfactions through purchasing from an ever expanding range of goods, then from the perspective of some twentieth century neo Marxists this development is regarded as producing greater opportunities for controlled and manipulated consumption. The expansion of capitalist production, especially after the boost received from scientific management and "Fordism" around the turn of the century, it's held, necessitated the construction of new markets and the "education" of publics to become consumers through advertising and other media. (p. 14)

In effect, Featherstone reiterates the tendency toward product diversification, promotion of new consumer goods and services, and consumption of the specific commodities (otherwise known as post-Fordism). The relationship between the creation and consumption of new products, leisure time, and cultural value is rather interesting.

As Schor (1991) observed in a discussion analyzing the decline of leisure time, leisure was commoditized into a diversified product incorporating many different goods and services. However, productivity increased, while leisure was transformed into a scarce commodity. Schor refers to increased productivity as measured by working time. She observes that the level of productivity has more than doubled. Schor claims that, "we could now produce our 1948 standard of living (measured in terms of marketed goods and services) in less than half the time it took in that year." She claims that production efficiency ensures that workers can enjoy more leisure time while producing the same industrial output (p. 2).

Schor continues her argument by noting that the narrowing of time for leisure-time pursuits has a significant impact on the marketing of specific alternatives. Schor states that productivity growth has been lower since 1984 but still averages just over 1 percent a year. Her point is that working hours have steadily risen over the last two decades. Americans continually spend a significant portion of their earnings on diversified food and clothing alternatives. Many Americans are also spending what they haven't yet earned (pp. 2–3).

Schor then points out that the American standard of living is the highest in the world (p. 3).[1] Schor also observes that increased work hours result when manufacturers seek even more productivity, and workers need additional income for satisfying consumer debt and increased spending. Leisure (or the consumption of free time) is sharply curtailed and therefore becomes a more valuable commodity. Schor also claims that free time is a scarce commodity. Americans seemingly "crowd expensive leisure spending into smaller periods of time":

On the other hand, the "market" for free time hardly exists in America. With few exceptions, employers (the sellers) don't offer the chance to trade off income gains for a shorter work days or the occasional sabbatical. They just pass on income, in the form of annual pay raises or bonuses, or if granting increased vacation or personal days, usually do so unilaterlly. Employees rarely have the chance to exercise an actual choice about how they will spend their productivity dividend. The closest substitute for a "market in leisure" is the travel and other leisure industries that advertise products to occupy or free time. But this indirect effect has been weak, as consumers crowd expensive leisure spending into smaller periods of time. (p. 3)

Schor staunchly believes that the decline in leisure time places a greater premium on the limited time that American workers can enjoy. Unfortunately, the choices generally reflect involuntary consumer decisions. Workers inevitably utilize alternatives provided by the consumer culture in enjoying their limited leisure time.

Leisure is transformed into another commodity product. Consumption is commoditized in terms of its cultural value. Featherstone (1991) offers an interesting Marxist interpretation of the relationship between leisure and exchange value. He claims that the products of culture are presented to a "manipulated mass who participate in an ersatz mass-produced commodity culture targeted at the lowest common denominator" (p. 14).

As Featherstone claims, the postmodern interpretation of leisure and culture emphasized the view that "emphasis shifts from production to reproduction, to the endless reduplication of signs, images and simulations through the media which effaces the distinction between the image and reality" (p. 15). Consumer society becomes cultural as social life becomes deregulated and social relationships become more variable.

The postmodern view of consumer credit and consumer culture views credit cards as variable symbols useful in extending cultural capital (or credit cards as quantifiable financial instruments). The credit card extends the acquisition of cultural experience by making the unaffordable "affordable." Few people will express surprise at the notion that credit cards act as symbols enabling us to consume either other symbols or consumer and popular culture.

"TOURISM" AND THE DEVELOPMENT OF CONSUMER CULTURE

Experiences made accessible through consumer credit dictate a new realm of social reality. Consumer culture bridges the culture bound elements of our sensual society with economic propriety. Each tourist or lifestyle device examined in this section embodies cultural experiences that are facilitated or made accessible through consumer credit.

In some cases, experiences are marketed as tangible products. Some examples of cultural products intended for consumer consumption include the proliferation of economically profitable theme parks. Zukin's (1991) examination of DisneyWorld as a cultural manifestation planned for economic gain is one such example. One could also apply these ideas as a rationale for why Jim and Tammy Faye Bakker's Heritage USA was the second "most" attended theme park in the United States.[2]

Other examples include the development of telephone sex, psychic hot lines, fantasy suites, Las Vegas, and the appeal of Disney World as the quintessential theme park. The above products are assessed through the utilization of consumer credit. All of these parasocial services compose cultural capital as interpreted on an experiential level. The consumption of these tourist areas or emergent manifestations of cultural expression is marketed as a reflection of emergent cultural experience.

Telephone sex consists of an essential escape from everyday stress into sexual experiences cloaked with assured safe sex (Klein, 1983). The new psychic hot line phenomenon also succeeds because communication between average persons and "experts" allows for an antidote to the uncertainty surrounding people in their everyday lives.

The economic facilitation of consumer credit promotes the accessibility of these niche-marketed cultural alternatives. The link between actual tourist sites and parasocial services rests with a consumer desire for real or figurative escape within an ever-changing social world. Both telephone sex and the telepsychic services were successful because they fulfilled a perceived consumer need through a carefully planned marketing promotion. Las Vegas and DisneyWorld, both popular tourist locations, met consumer desires through marketing promotion and emphasis on intangible consumer desires (e.g., the fulfillment of cultural fantasies or the immediate consumption of heavily marketed cultural images, such as the opportunity to attend world-renowned stage spectacles or actually meet legendary Disney characters).

These artifacts, as derived from a postmodern society, are meaningless unless we reflect on the socio-historical process leading to current cultural expression. The original relationship between marketing and consumer purchasing decisions consisted of advertising goods for sale. Greatly expanded manufacturing capacity and consumer desires led to more choices within the marketplace. The post-Fordist era ushered in an era of diversified products and choices available for consumer acquisition. The cultural desires prompting acquisition of the produced goods and services was facilitated through the introduction of installment credit and eventually the distribution of credit cards.

Instantaneous consumer choices fit right into the postmodern conception of American society. Consumers can utilize credit cards in lieu of available cash. Theme parks, telephone services, or even a meal at McDonald's is immediately affordable.

Contemporary society is a place noted for ever-changing cultural patterns. Advertised products are the result of predetermined marketing efforts designed to pinpoint what consumers will purchase. One example of this is a device known as "The Club." It fits on the automobile steering wheel and prevents auto theft. The Club was phenomenally successful on introduction into the marketplace. Since then, there have been numerous imitations produced by competing companies. The original manufacturer countered with the marketing of the same product in various colors. The last step was successful in redefining the product according to appearance instead of original utility.[3]

Human experience works according to the same principle. The introduction of a telephone sex service, telephone psychic service, or the original Disneyland brought forth cultural alternatives enabling the formation of redefined consumer cultural experiences. Consumer credit as an economic resource facilitates the immediate acquisition of knowledge, parasocial experience, or a temporary escape from the realities of everyday life. The imagery associated with telephone conversation, environmental stimuli, and interactional cues from telephone services and actual surroundings in theme parks or malls encourages exposure to the product of human experience and encouraged consumption. The inevitable outcome of niche marketing is a myriad number of personal choices reflecting products gaining cultural acceptance at any given time.

Tourism is intertwined with the development of consumer culture. Acceptance of the postmodern condition wherein cultural choices and consumer purchasing choices shift over time characterizes the transitory nature of American society. The formation of cultural capital results in consumable social alternatives immediately unaffordable without various credit instruments. Economic power in the form of credit cards and installment credit provides a means for consuming the latest products, trends, or experiences.

In a sense, we are all "strangers in a strange land" (a cliche taken from a popular science fiction novel written by Robert Heinlein, 1959). The cultural objects or environments that we consume give meaning to our lives. In effect, we are reminded of the philosophy espoused in *Field of Dreams*. "You build it and they will come" is an appropriate collorary to the development of the tourist industry. Cultural events provide a context of references shared or sought by numerous people. Americans define their lives in terms of a special experience enjoyed while on vacation, a meaningful dinner with friends, mutual activities enjoyed in a unique place, or shared interaction in the company of other people or through the auspices of a telephone.[4]

Veblen (1899/1967) was correct in positing that the consumption of particular goods or things was conducive to building status formations. MacCannell (1989) takes the analysis one step further in referring to people as fellow travelers seeking everything that life offers. MacCannell suggests that the "tourist" is "one of the best models available for modern man in general."[5]

In effect, the tourist represents how an average person makes his or her way through everyday life. MacCannell imposes an anthropological view of social existence based upon structural analysis. Tourist attractions represent "an unplanned topology of structure that provides direct access to the modern consciousness or 'world view' " (p. 2).

In other words, tourism (as facilitated by enhanced consumer credit opportunities) serves to structure the creation of social meaning. MacCannell utilizes formulations of Goffman, Garfinkel, Veblen, Marx, Simmel, and other social theorists in demonstrating how experience, rather than Veblen's reliance on social class, dictates the social reality of everyday life.

Further, MacCannell compares tourist attractions with the "religious symbolism of primitive peoples" (p. 2). He is basically viewing modernity as "disorganized fragments, alienating, wasteful, violent, superficial, unplanned, unstable and unauthentic." The worldwide shift in national governments incorporate nostalgia and a search for authenticity. MacCannell sees "the empirical and ideological expansion of modern society to be intimately linked in diverse ways to modern mass leisure, especially to international tourism and sightseeing" (p. 3).

MacCannell places particular significance in the structure of social space. His analysis invokes Goffman's model of everyday activity. MacCannell repeatedly refers to Goffman's (1959) conception of front stage and back stage as the basis of understanding everyday social reality. Tourist activities are centered around relating with "the natives" in a quest for "authentic experiences, perceptions and insights" (MacCannell, 1989, p. 103). The tourist is trapped within an endless process wherein the truth about native populations is illusive. Economic instruments (in the form of consumer credit) aid and abet in the perpetual search for tangible social meaning through the acquisition of actual or parasocial experience in the form of cultural capital.

Economic formation and the implicit shifts emphasizing consumption and experience as a tangible product incorporate the development of consumer culture. Tourism, as facilitated by available consumer credit, enables the consumption of hitherto unaffordable experiences. The consumer culture transforms places or experiences into symbols for intrinsic cultural capital. Peer value or self-fulfillment is associated with accessing an interpersonal phone line service or visiting places such as Las Vegas or Disney World.

TELEPHONE SEX AS A CULTURAL MANIFESTATION

Telephone sex is a perfect example of postmodern experience dependent on cultural acceptance and technological advances. The economic system enables the collection of revenue through sophisticated telephone computer software or credit card billing techniques.

The telephone sex phenomenon began in 1983. An average of 500,000 people per day dialed popular New York City numbers. These telephone callers did not learn the time, weather, horoscope, daily prayer, or any jokes. The material consisted of women (and sometimes men) engaged in an explicitly sexual situation. The taped messages escalated from the description of sexual activity to an ultimate sexual "climax." This is selectively termed "Dial a Porn," "living centerfolds," or simulated telephone sex—depending on description by the press, general public, or entrepreneurs providing the service. Later telephone sex services concentrated on live women reciting scripted routines in return for agreed-upon fees.

The first part of the discussion offered here deals with the sociological disposition of the original taped telephone sex service as a postmodern development. The service, as originally initiated by *High Society* magazine, is considerably different from the live "Dial a Fantasy" services spontaneously offered by women upon ascertainment of credit card payment arrangements. Both phenomena share many of the same sociological implications. A later discussion of live telephone sex services will embody the nature of social experience as a consumable form of symbolic capital.

The general analysis of telephone sex vehicles incorporates a basic overview of American society. Many people desperately "reach out" for taboo or socially restricted experiences. This is where experiential sexual sensation fits into a postmodern context. Some individuals may claim that symbolic sexual discourse is a form of escape without the physical confines of a Disneyland or a DisneyWorld. The telephone, as a form of "safe sex" is the vehicle rather than a situation suggested by physical props. The converse situation, wherein social construction of human experience is achieved through surrounding architectural design as an enabling device, is dealt with at a later point in the analysis.

The reader must understand the reasons for the formation of these industrial initiatives, some provided examples demonstrating the effectiveness of telephone sex as symbolic experience and how technological development embodies the institutionalization of postmodern experience. The repression of sexuality as stressed by Freud (1914) leads people toward fulfillment of these forbidden yearnings. These questionable telephone services, as provided by innovators offering a scarce commodity in return for profit, satisfy the needs of some people (Bell, 1953; Merton, 1968). We need only refer to prostitution as transacted in many midtown or business districts within cities around the country (Winick and Kinsie, 1971).

One could say that society "triggers the seeds of its own moral downfall." Everyday social interaction holds the challenge of enticing but unobtainable illusions (Lefebvre, 1971; Marcuse, 1964). Human sexual urges are subsumed within the family and other institutionally constraining arrangements. Social behavior is also systematically shaped through education, advertising, and other social influences (Goffman, 1981).

The postmodern view of society tends to view sexual expression as a reflection of changing social mores. The recent proliferation of upscale strip clubs and the celebration of well-endowed women is a recent manifestation of entertainment reflecting an open view of parasocial sexual experience. Blatant sexuality was formerly reserved for pornographic movies or specific magazines featuring nudity or sexual acts.

The new attitudes and frequent consumption of sexual expression are popularized by increased niche marketing within the sex industry. Sex is now a more acceptable product that can be sold as a consumable experience and billed on a credit card. In the past, television and radio content offered sanitized versions of graphic sex sequences and specifically forbidden scatological language. David Letterman succinctly projected this puritan influence in the now-famous phrase "It feels so good, it must be illegal." Our moral values are justified through invoking "the old-fashioned (or traditional) way." We are in the twentiety century, but many of the societal attitudes toward sex are rooted in the late 1800s or the early part of the current century.

Men and women seek relief from the societal restraints influencing our visible everyday presentation of self (Goffman, 1959). Suggestiveness is intensified with nervous laughter and blushing in public upon overhearing obscene stories. Intensity of commitment toward our personalized gender identity is expressed through suggestion of fantasy rather than physical actions.

In fact, numerous critics have contended that we are living in an age of narcissism (Lasch, 1978). Charles Reich (1974) would claim that we are the "me generation" grown into a social value system stressing a more personal and conventional gratification. Suggestive sexual telephone messages play on this social phenomenon. One can almost paraphrase the late Timothy Leary's much-quoted pro-LSD statement as "Dial up—listen in—get turned on."

Several factors set the stage for the emergence of telephone sex. Ambiguous moral standards and innovative developments are two of these factors. Both factors are the offshoot of a postmodern era wherein sex is transformed from a social taboo into an everyday cultural product.

In fact, new communications techniques play an important part in this transformation. Everyday social functions are increasingly absorbed in an encompassing communications revolution. One need only examine "Dial a Date" and "Citizen Radio Prostitution" as examples of the last point. Both phenomenon are overshadowed by massive acceptance of the talk radio format (Avery and Ellis, 1979). We can interact with one another either through directly broadcast conversation with strangers or the vicarious experience of "eavesdropping" via our own radio.[6]

A brief discussion of "Dial a Date" and "CB Radio Prostitution" will amplify this last point. "Dial a Date" was initiated as an attempt to facilitate communication among individuals. The *Village Voice* and other newspapers or magazines across the country advertise recorded dating services. Single men and women can call specific telephone numbers and hear either men, women, homosexuals, or ethnic groups describing themselves. Each person is identified by a number. Callers can communicate with a selected person or persons by sending several dollars for the privilege of having their letters forwarded. Both the "advertisers" and the date seekers pay a fee for the service. The attraction of this mechanized dating service is the safe introduction between two individuals.[7]

The process is taken one step further by the introduction of "CB Radio Prostitution" (Klein and Luxenburg, 1983). Researchers are provided a unique opportunity for analyzing interaction. Either truckers or prostitutes can initiate the social selection process through carefully measured talk. Truckers and prostitutes establish enough rapport through brief conversation to warrant a personal meeting and discussion of specific prices. Sexual activity follows these carefully constructed social efforts. The conversation has no restrictions other than the desires of both parties. There is no "gatekeeper" (such as a radio talk show host or formal call screener) to censor the conversation. Everything said by both parties is taken with a grain of salt as "regulars" monitoring the channel know what to expect.[8]

Both "Dial a Date" and "CB Radio Prostitution" are predicated on a system of ambiguous social morals and the potential innovation presented by this new opportunity structure. The changes in sexual values from conservative in nature during the 1950s, liberal in the 1960s and the early 1970s, and a mixture of both in the 1970s up through the present have produced major ideological changes (*Time*, 1984). The "baby boom" generation has matured into a population cohort typically averaging from the mid- to upper-thirties. Various changes in female lifestyle (from workplace participation to having babies later in life) have equalized or given women more power over their personal lives. The life status change is reflected in a freer exchange of views between dating and marital partners. Sex is much more open for this generation than those sexually mature adults in the 1950s. The roles of men and women are not as well delineated as in the past.

Innovation and this new social opportunity are key factors in this realistic transformation. Gradual development of social inventions and their subsequent effect on the social structure have produced a profound effect on American society (Aronson, 1979). The telephone, talk radio formats, and CB radios are three communications inventions producing major changes in the daily interaction between individuals and society. Merton (1968) is indirectly indicating that illegitimate opportunities often arise out of transitory social or technological factors. Thus, telephone, radio, and citizen band radio communication are potentially co-optable for expression of sexual ideas between two or more adults.

We can subsequently translate these notions into a consideration of the issues underlying telephone sex. Ironically, the legal system acted in legitimizing telephone sex as an acceptable option in the niche marketing of sexual experience. A long-standing antitrust case against AT&T was settled with a court-ordered divestiture. Harold Green, a US federal judge, directed a two-year, $80 billion divestiture of 22 regional companies from the parent conglomerate (*Time*, 1983; *New York Times*, 1982). Telephone service, long-distance calls, local service, and equipment manufacture were subdivided into independent entities. As a result, many public telephone numbers were decontrolled and leased to private businesses through a systematic lottery.[9]

Companies competed for these telephone numbers. In January 1983, *High Society* magazine was awarded one of these outlets. New York Telephone was obliged to supply the phone line service. *High Society* magazine and other winning businesses used the windfall for public relations purposes. For example, several businesses sponsored horse racing results or beauty tips. The proceeds were subject to sharing between the telephone company and the private businesses. Where the telephone company previously used the more than $4 million profit for offsetting local phone rates, the revenue was redistributed with $.07 per call retained by New York Telephone and $.02 per call going to the private business (Morality in Media, Inc., 1984; *Philadelphia Inquirer*, 1983).

There is a dimension of pornography pertaining to the Dial a Porn phenomenon. The *High Society* "living centerfold" service incorporates some of the features associated with pornography. Dial a Porn is an "aural" extension of the "pornographic marketplace." We have a disembodied voice instead of peep shows or rap booths. The totality is equivalent to an aural rap booth without a woman's physical presence.[10] Ball and Lilly (1981) describe how regular motel customers are aware of available pornographic movies. Similarly, Dial a Porn phone callers expect suggestive scenarios. The fantasy element is not dissimilar to Dudley Moore's lust for forbidden dreams in the film *10*.

The fantasy element is clearly present in Dial a Porn telephone monologues. Callers are presented with simulated sexual activities suggesting masturbation, cunnilingus, fellatio, anilingus, or excretory functions.[11] (All four segments cited in the endnote include females acting as "seductresses.") The female initiates the sexual situation and "turns on" a fictional partner (anyone listening to the recording). An initial sexual situation is proposed, followed by suggestive sexual activity and the female's sexual climax. The male's ego and sex potency are stressed. The conclusion of the 57-second monologue features an invitation to call back at another time. Most messages end with an advertisement for live sex calls (arranged through credit card payment).

CALLING FOR PSYCHIC ADVICE

The advent of billing through the assignment of "900 numbers" facilitated the provision of various consumer experiences. An interested person can obtain sports scores, horoscopes, medical advice, and many other forms of information.

One service is the provision of psychic advice administered over the phone. The Psychic Friends Service Network was the first such service. As promoted by an infomercial (a half-hour-length television commercial masquerading as a regular television program), Dionne Warwick introduced celebrities and other people served by psychic advisees. The psychic advice generally costs from $3 to $5 per minute. More than a half dozen other such services followed in the wake of the Psychic Friends Service Network.[12]

Psychic telephone services fulfill a particular need. People are always facing uncertainty in life. The telephone psychics ostensibly offer solace and guidance in coping with everyday situations. Individuals are utilizing credit cards or automatic telephone billing credit in accessing experience. According to Maury Povich and other talk programs, some individuals accumulate thousands of dollars in charges to psychic advice phone lines.[13] Credit cards or automatic billing (a form of revolving credit) facilitates the everyday use of the psychic services. The consequence of established psychic telephone services is an accumulation of consumer debt. The end-product is another service transformed into a habitual need.

Telephone psychics compose a form of cultural capital supported by economic institutions. The advent of modern technology permits an individualized dispersal of information. Prior to instituting telephone service, psychics were available primarily through private contact.

Psychic services are a form of communication within a continually shifting social framework. The parasocial elements, buttressed by the use of credit for eventual payment, constitute a form of societal entertainment. An information exchange through electronic means signals the emergence of "tourists" seeking out a "path in life." Tourists want to believe the reality of psychic advice as much as they subscribe to the sexual imagery provided by telephone sex services.

In the long run, psychic telephone services are another form of fantasy experience available to travelers seeking reaffirmation of a prevailing social order. Niche marketing permits the public dissemination of information on our personal lives. Information is offered as a commodity available for public consumption. In turn, the purchased information is instrumental in the continued construction of social identity.

We must also consider a physical—rather than strictly information-driven—environment wherein the setting transcends the symbolic nature of the cultural setting in the structuring of human experience. Bourdieu (1984), Harvey (1989), and others might agree that the cultural views expressed in such surroundings are made accessible through specialized marketing and a planned economic strategy.

Tourism and expert marketing are intricately linked. Credit cards are an inevitable and important element in tourism. Tourist needs for satisfying hotel bills, paying for expensive floor shows, charging food and drinks, shopping at high-scale shopping malls, and obtaining gambling funds from ComCash or another competing bank cash system are all fulfilled through the use of credit cards. Consumer credit also enhances the tourist experience through encouraging escapism when the tourist does not have immediate financial concerns.

FANTASY SUITES: ROOMS WITH A VIEW

Telephone fantasy experiences and telepsychics are various dimensions of cultural expression made possible through technological means and provided through a niche marketing system. Fantasy Suites are another form of marketed human experience. The desire for spending leisure time in unusual and previously unaffordable places is facilitated through the use of credit cards. People can try new experiences without the fear of immediate consumer debt.

The considerable cost of fantasy suites, along with the other experiences described in this chapter, is efficiently handled without the use of cash payments. In fact, most hotels will insist on credit cards rather than immediate cash. The Fantasy Suite location in the Midwest and a steep $100 per night necessitate credit card use. Salaries in the Midwest are lower than the national average. The Fantasy Suite accommodation rate is more typical of the East or West Coast than the Midwest.

Hotel accommodations are basically reminiscent of the Fordist era. Americans quickly discover one disconcerting fact through their cumulative millions of miles spent on the road: All hotel rooms seem alike. Hotel chains owned and managed by Howard Johnson, Hilton, Sharaton, Holiday Inn, and countless other nationwide corporations are basically intended for the casual or business traveler. Each hotel room contains the obligatory bed, dresser, Gideon Bible, television set, and writing desk. The decor is usually middle American, featuring hotel room walls adorned with portraits of Americana.

Most people are on the road seeking new places and unique adventures. Many locales are creating attractions targeted at gaining the attention of an ever-curious American public. Some hotels (such as the Waldorf-Astoria, Fairmount, and Fountainbleu) offer unique experiences through special decor and a marketed image.

Hotel rooms also have an alternative connotation in the cultural history of the American society. Some individuals associate hotels with the ability to engage in certain sexual activities not possible in their own homes. Ball and Lilly (1983) coauthored a now classic piece explaining the function of deviance in the hotel setting. The so called no tell motel accommodating illicit lovers or businessmen consorting with prostitutes, has become legendary. These notorious motels charge by the hour and permit the interchange of cash payment and sexual services.

Entrepreneurs seize on the desire to fulfill sexual fantasies, whether in the setting of a downtown hotel, an obscure motel, a trucking vehicle, or another mutually agreeable locale. Klein and Luxenburg (1981, 1982) explored the public nature of interpersonal transactions as negotiated by prostitutes and truckers over citizen band airwaves; then performed in trucks situated on interstate highways, at truck stops, or at motels off main thoroughfares. Their research revealed that forms of sexuality (and sensuality in the case of conveying meaning through encoded CB radio communication) are refocused in the context of accommodating a mobile American society.

A post-Fordist atmosphere offering nontradition experience pervades specific hotel settings in a much more subtle way. In 1985, a hotel chain headquartered in Minneapolis, Minnesota, acquired a former Holiday Inn located in a mid-western city. The management team experimented with a concept they termed "fantasy suites." The fantasy suites were hotel rooms designed around specific themes. The first suites, predecessors of the 24 rooms existent at the time of this research, included Infinity, Captain's Quarters, Eastern Winds, Cupid's Corner, Space Odyssey, and LeCave. These suites, which will be described in more detail, are designed around specific concepts appealing to particular individuals or couples.

Analysis of this phenomenon is undertaken on two levels. The first level is analysis of American culture and how we define our lives through imagined roles or images. Niche marketing is effective in researching, operationalizing, and transforming experience into cultural capital. Sensual meaning is translated into commercial appeal as depicted within literature, films, television, magazines, and deliberately targeted advertising efforts. An advertised product finds its eventual audience through a rationally calculated media display.

The second level will take us through an analysis of questionnaire responses completed by a ramdom sampling at one of the fantasy suite hotels. An undergraduate research assistant and myself arranged for the distribution of in-room surveys asking guests about their socio-economic status, percpetions of the various fantasy suites, and reasons for choosing a specialty room rather than the standard suite. The hotel management placed 230 questionnaires within the 14 fantasy suites in a two-week period during late May and early June 1989. Sixty-two completed questionnaires were collected by the hotel staff (constituting a response rate approximately reaching 25 percent). Upon inspection, 60 of these survey responses were complete enough for further analysis. The aggregate responses detailed below indicate how the introduction of an attractively marketed experiential product gains acceptance in spite of predisposed attitudes toward sexual content.

Sensuality and Cultural Conditioning

It is possible that more average persons are accepting sensuality as a facet of everyday life.[14] The Puritan influence, as originated in the fifteenth century, stressed aesthetic values rather than temptation. Hard work and devotion to work were components of the preferred lifestyle. These values were transformed into a systematic ethos subsequently termed the Protestant ethic (Weber, 1902/1958). The Protestant ethic, as discussed by Weber, deemphasized materialistic values in favor of elective affinity (or human action for the purpose of achieving success in the next life).

How do we deal with the emphasis on sensuality throughout the twentieth century? The Protestant ethic was endorsed in name only, as opposed to practicing its other-worldly ideal. Several factors account for the selling of sensuality as an everyday commodity: the rise of capitalism, evolution of mass communication, and the industrialization of American society. The rise of capitalism was a major force in the alteration of sexual behavior. Sexuality, or then notion that alternate means of recreation and self-expression were legitimate, became marketed as an acceptable release. Conformity was achieved at the expense of constant economic and social pressure. The movers and shakers of the industrial sector realized that workers needed a diversion from everyday pressures.

Thus, sexuality became condoned as a behavioral solution for the ongoing discontent. Bell (1976b) argued that capitalism could not function as a mechanistic process when cultural value structures undermined and altered individual responses. Cultural contradictions within capitalism weakened the underpinning established by the tenets of the Protestant Ethic. Thus, the ideal of hard work and economic sacrifice competed with physical and emotional release during leisure periods. One use of discretionary funds expended in this manner was directed toward curiosity regarding officially forbidden sexual expression. Many people sought out sexual release, whether in the vicarious form of films and literature or as part of an individualized lifestyle. Illicit sexual affairs, children conceived in illegitimate relationships, and the recognition of sexuality as an emotional outlet could be seen as expressions of this desire.

Not coincidentally, entrepreneurs came along and offered a form of cultural capital that the public wanted but could not obtain from established businessmen. Industrial advances and technological change (e.g., videocassette recorders, cable television, computers, photo and video duplicating processes) facilitated the marketing of such sexually oriented products. The primary interest of employers and government (or ruling-class interests within the Marxian means of production) was directed toward keeping the masses satisfied. Leisure time was maximized through utilization of discretionary income for pleasurable pursuits (Ewen, 1976).[15]

Sexuality was safely manufactured through media and entrepreneurial devices directed toward profit-producing activities. Consumers chose the vehicles where they could express their sexual desires in a safe atmosphere. The sexual connotation of these outlets (whether self-improvement products or locations facilitating a safe ventilation of life's frustrations) was quickly accepted whether vicariously through television or experimentally in specific settings designed for that purpose.

Capitalist efforts toward accumulating more wealth or influence can take on a "hit or miss" quality. One theoretical explanation offers the assertion that exposing oneself to cultural expression is a voluntary act. A surprising confirmation of the postmodern perspective comes from Michael Schudson (1984), who challenges he assertion of overall manipulation in asserting that capitalism works as an economic and social phenomenon. The individual is probably as responsible as the media in creating this effect. The successful marketing of particular products encourages reinforcement of the already expressed public attitudes in previous promotions or advertising campaigns. Sensuality, as utilized in advertising, is useful in the incorporation of pleasure into the marketing of ordinary products.

Any heightened effect of capitalism as an economic and social system or a cultural phenomenon is further strengthened by mass media effects. Several points are vital in the development of an understanding of factors supporting the fantasy suite concept. First, mass media act as a force diffusing expression of acceptable lifestyle trends among the masses. The so-called hypodermic effect in which people experience social stimuli and incorporate the positive effect into their lifestyles is vital in this analysis. Basic human drives or urges are satisfied through the suggestiveness of media cues that may be directed at our ego or superego (Blumler and Katz, 1974).

These cues can range from the merits of hard work and discipline to wanton pleasure through devices facilitating sexual expression. This is where the contradictions posed in Bell's 1976 analysis become operative. The work ethic conflicts with the need for stimulating the economy through the development of consumer credit. The comingling of these two polar ranges creates confusion and the crisis created by an emphasis on consumerism to the detriment of capitalist production. In the case of an analysis sufficient for explaining the fantasy suite phenomenon, it would suffice to indicate that sensuality is accompanied with marked sexual content as a direct (or indirect) product. Advertising, television content, popular magazines, films, and other forms of popular culture are more attractive than hard work and discipline. The balance is shifted, and priorities can become slanted toward sexuality as a constant in every aspect of our lives.

A central point presented in succeeding pages emphasizes that sensuality, as used in a marketing ploy for creating acceptance of new products, becomes a commodity overshadowing the products themselves. Experience, rather than the deterministic nature of some economic or political institutions, dictates cultural development. The traditional Frankfurt School view argued otherwise. Marcuse (1964) and Lefebvre (1971) argued that we are transformed into an expression of the values intuited by commodities and their subjective place in our lives. Consumers of this culture become the sum total of their experiences and the typification discussed by Alfred

Schutz and created by the overall social system (Natanson, 1964). In simpler terms, the old phrase "you are what you eat" summarizes the impact of this socialization pattern upon our lives. In effect, they attempt to have it both ways.

The process does not end with the evolution of mass communications that accompanies the rise of capitalism. Industrialism in American society is partially explainable through an understanding of the processes initiated by capitalism. First, advances in industrial production of leisure time pursuits are enabled through social invention. Social inventions are devices which aid commercial development and have a social effect upon our lives. In general, social inventions are innovations facilitating the opening of the marketplace and new options aimed at consumer interest. For example, Aronson (1979) argued that the telephone had such an effect. The business applications are obvious and the Dial-a-Porn phenomenon is one example of the uses and gratification approach operating on a social level. The credit card, and consumer credit, represent a system wherein the same effect is achieved through instant rather than deferred gratification.

The automobile is an important example of how social inventions have shaped everyday lifestyles. Henry Ford, in addition to providing more employment through imposition of the assembly line, recognized the social extension of the automobile. Ford could relate the invention to his own workers with the aid of built-in incentives such as increased wages, shorter work hours and installment purchase plans. In effect, Ford was creating a market through enhanced leisure time and affordable.[16]

The automobile was also vital in the consumer credit revolution and in explaining why the Fantasy Suite concept is successful. People gradually gained the wherewithal for expanding their travel plans within a larger area. The automobile and subsequent highway construction acted as a passport to areas beyond immediate residential communities. Spending power earned through accumulation of discretionary income was applicable toward leisure time pursuits.

A major industry consisting of shopping malls, rest areas and hotel/motel complexes capitalized upon the millions of motorists en route toward new residences or embarking on vacation travels. A new duality emerges with the growth of automobile use and the residual transportation amenities. These two factors are 1) the creation of a new subculture and 2) the social effect of the new subculture. First, America's love affair with the automobile spurred increase of the hotel/motel business just as the existence of these immediate "homes away from home" made automobile use more convenient.

These aspects, along with the expansion of interstate highways, made interstate travel a more desirable alternative. The hotel/motel complexes and other highway attractions had a social effect upon people utilizing those choices. On one level, attractions such as the West Bend FantaSuite hotel (located in West Bend, Wisconsin) offer a cathartic antidote in counteracting everyday stresses and pressures. On another level, these Fantasy Suites ostensibly offer lifestyle alternatives not available in another hometown or location. These lifestyle choices are expressed in changing the immediate atmosphere experienced by hotel guests.

General Background of the Fantasy Suite Concept

The Fantasy Suite concept was originated in 1985. At that time, the hotel management group decided to experiment with offering rooms which had alternative themes and decor. Most of the rooms offered either a jacuzzi or a waterbed as the centerpoint of the suite. The rest of the story has become history. The suites were subsequently installed at five other hotels throughout Wisconsin, Indiana, Iowa and Minnesota. The hotel chain renamed each of these places in 1988 as FantaSuite hotels (*New York Times*, October 13, 1988).

All 24 suites are generally reserved three months in advance for weekend stays and approximately two months in advance for weekday occupancy. Construction of each suite can cost up to $100,000 and the room rates are over $100 per night for most suites. Free tours are offered each Saturday and Sunday at 2:15 p.m. The rooms are opened for general inspection of the public and the tour usually attracts between 50–100 people.

The first suites were originally installed on a trial basis at the West Bend Fantasuite Hotel. The specific themes for the first six suites were Space Odyssey, LeCave, Infinity, Captain's Quarters, Eastern Winds and Cupid's Corner.[17]

The most popular suites are Space Odyssey, Northern Lights, The Continental, Igloo II and Caesar's Court. Space Odyssey was a space capsule surrounded by a moonscape. Northern Lights consists of an igloo, hot tub bordered by mirrors and a 10 sided waterbed. The Continental is furnished with an authentic 1964 Lincoln Continental, wet bar, wide screen TV, and jacuzzi with mirrors. Igloo II is a duplicate of Northern Lights. Lastly, Caesar's Court is a reproduction of Caesar's Villa. A hand painted mural provides atmosphere along with a king size, step-up bed, fountain and sensuous Roman bath.[18]

The most popular Fantasuites are those furnished with jacuzzi and waterbed features. Nightly room rates on those suites usually near or exceed $100 per night on weekdays and exceed $100 on weekends. Check-in is at 4 p.m. and check-out is 12 noon the next day. According to information gathered from personnel at the hotel, people enter the room and pre-order room service for dinner and the next morning's breakfast. The jacuzzi goes on first and other activities are subject to the choice and discretion of the hotel guests.

Guest Attitudes Regarding the Fantasuite Experience

Background information volunteered by the Marketing Director for the West Bend Fantasuite hotel provided an introduction into the Fantasy Suite phenomena.[19] A questionnaire soliciting information on several categories was devised as a result of information obtained in that interview. These factors included: a) socio-economic status factors (age, gender, education, occupation, income, race, marital status, and religion); b) relationship of people staying in the Fantasy Suite rooms; c) where people were traveling from; d) why they chose a Fantasy Suite rather than a regular hotel room; e) the suite chosen, whether it was their first choice and why they chose it; f) any other Fantasuites utilized in the past; g) what they liked and disliked about their experience; h) where they heard about the Fantasuite concept; and i) any suggestions for other Fantasuites.

The first section of the questionnaire focused on socio-economic variables. The socio-economic variables describe an interesting and diverse sampling population. Overall, the age of males occupying a fantasy suite ranged from 21–53, with both median and mean approximately 32. Female ages ranged from 20–38, median was 26 and the mean was 27. Forty males responded on the survey form. Thirty two were married and eight were single. Twenty seven females gave their views on the Fantasy Suites. Twenty four females were married and three were "single." The reader must realize that some couples recorded dual responses on their survey forms. We recorded those responses as coupled except for the specification of age, gender, education, occupation, income, marital status and religion.

The age and gender distinctions indicate that most couples were married. This finding confirms the observation that most people taking the Fantasy Suite tour were married and at least in their mid-twenties. We noticed two interesting cases involving age and marital status within the various survey responses. In one instance, a 20 year old, single female shared a Fantasy Suite with her boyfriend. This is interesting because Fantasy Suite guests must be 21 unless married. But exceptions are not uncommon since a female college student admitted that she had shared a Fantasuite with her boyfriend on two occasions. In a second instance, two men shared the Space Odyssey Fantasy Suite. One of them, a 31 year old male complained that they were given a cool reception at the hotel desk. Both men traveled from a nearby urban area and the respondent claimed that he followed the pagan religion.

An interesting pattern emerged when examining the educational background of the Fantasy Suite patrons. We were able to ascertain the educational backgrounds of 38 males and 24 females. The male respondents' educational background consisted of the following categories: High School Dropout, 1; High School Graduate, 13; Some College, 14; College Graduate, 5; Graduate Education, 5. Female respondents reported the following educational levels: High School Dropout, 0; High School Graduate, 6; Some College, 11; College Graduate, 7; Graduate Education, 0.[20]

The men and women in this survey held occupations confirming traditional gender stereotypes and income levels. Income levels ranged from $6,000–$100,000 for males (we made adjustments for this extreme income level) and female salaries ranged from $1,000–$55,000 (we could discard the lower range salary and still notice lower yearly earnings). An averaging of reported salaries yielded a mean of $30,017.54. But we minimized the one extreme male income, reported by an operations supervisor. The corrected average indicated an income approximating $25,000. Salaries were generally higher for urban dwellers than local town inhabitants. Urban residents were generally more educated and working in professional positions. Small town inhabitants worked in factory settings and earned approximately $30,000 on the highest level.

As indicated in our discussion of marital status, most rooms were occupied by married couples. There were eight single men and three single women accounted for in our survey. Ages for those couples, with the exception of two men sharing a suite, consisted of the following: male, 31 (female age unspecified); male, 27 (female age unspecified); male, 23 (age of fiance unspecified); female, 20 (age of boyfriend unspecified); male, 30 divorced (girlfriend's age unspecified) and male, 25 (fiance's age 30).[21]

Religious background reflected residential population demographic patterns. Lutheran and Catholic were the most prevalent religious backgrounds. Twenty nine FantaSuite patrons were Lutheran—17 males and 12 females. There were 21 Catholics—16 males and 6 females. Both Methodists were male. The remaining religious affiliations consisted of the following groups: Nondenominational, 2 (one male, one female); Baptist, 1 (male); Scientologist, 1 (female); and Presbyterian 1 (male).

The survey also included a question on why these people chose a Fantasy Suite instead of a traditional room. The perceivable reasons, ranked in order of mention on the questionnaires, appeared as follows: "different," 22; anniversary, 16; honeymoon, 6; romanticism, 6; gift, 3; birthday, 3; fun, 3; and adventure, 1. One person, a 37 year old female, wrote, "I think we need and deserve to do something special for ourselves at least once a year, this is it." Another female, 27, wrote, "We wanted something different." A female, 20, wrote that the Fantasy Suite was, "different, exciting, sexually stimulating." A couple, male, 25, and female, 24, wrote that the suites enabled them to "get away and relax." Other people mentioned such factors as intimacy, novelty and a different atmosphere.

We summarized the suites people chose, which suites were their actual first choices, and how many patrons received their choices through availability or preferences. Twenty five people indicated that the suite they occupied was their first choice or best available preference. Space Odyssey was the most popular first choice (ten people). Other first choices, ranked in order of preference, were Pearl Under the Sea (7); Northern Lights (5); Caesar's Court (3); LeCave (2); Klondike, Captain's Quarters, Cupid's Corner, Tepee, Infinity, The Continental, Jungle Safari, Igloo II, Treehouse (1).

Actual choices, as differentiated from suites that people generally settled for, were recorded as follows: Gambler, 6; LeCave, 5; Happy Days Cafe, Cupid's Corner, Tepee, Caesar's Court, 4; Klondike, Captain's Quarters, The Continental, Igloo II, 3; Dungeon, Pearl Under the Sea, Northern Lights, Jungle Safari, Wild West, 2; Space Odyssey, Viking, Tiajuana Jail, Infinity, Arabian Nights, Covered Wagon, Eastern Winds, Pharaoh's Tomb, 1.

One of the survey items asked whether the patrons had taken a public tour before choosing a particular suite. Forty seven people responded to this item. Twenty eight people had not taken a tour while nineteen people had actually went gone on a tour prior to their stay. Respondents taking the tour cited curiosity about the suites and comparison in making a choice. People not taking the tour cited the unavailability of the tour on that given day or that the suite recommendation had already come from a friend.

Respondents were asked where they heard about the Fantasy Suites. Referral sources, as ranked in order, consisted of the following: friends, 21; relatives, 5; work colleague, travel agent, 3; newspaper, Don Q Inn, radio, television, 2; husband, Omni Magazine, publicity upon original opening, hotel worker, previous patron, beautician, wife, National Enquirer, mother, travel magazine, pamphlet, 1.[22]

People have various reasons for choosing their suites. Many people claimed that their choice was the only one available. Others specifically stated that the chosen suite had an appealing atmosphere. Waterbed, jacuzzi, mirrors, stereo and specific decor (e.g., the red and black colors of Gambler, a heart shaped bed in Cupid's Corner, and the coffee cup jacuzzi in Happy Days Inn) were frequently cited factors for most suites. One Fantasuite patron stated that the room was, "away from home and they could stay in a room not similar to your bedroom."

Suite Suggestions

Respondents were asked if they had any suggestions for prospective Fantasy Suites. The West Bend Fantasuite Hotel and the five other hotels routinely include such requests on their room evaluation form. Individuals submitting an accepted concept receive a free night in the Fantasuite of their choice. We divided the suggestions into five categories: a) outdoors; b) beach; c) sports; d) romantic; e) recreational; and f) transportation. Nine suggestions were received in the outdoors category. These were wilderness camp (2), hunting camp (2), canal ride, fishing camp, ant farm, bee have and log cabin. The surrounding state offers excellent natural resources and people generally enjoy the outdoors. Thus, enhancement of a time spent in an outdoors setting is transferred into this environment. In fact, the hotel already has several successful suites stressing the outdoors.

The beach theme was also popular. Seven people mentioned various types of beach settings. These were beach themes: beach front, beach, Hawaii (2); and Cancun, Jamaica and Acapulco. People seemed to feel that the warm sand, surf and tropical climate are soothing atmospheric conditions.

The most popular category was romance. There were eleven suggestions in this category. They consisted of a desert scene (with tent bed); bridal suite; volcano; in the clouds (literally); an old fashioned room (equipped with fireplace, cozy log cabin and antique decor); a hay loft; a fantasy island; a pirate ship; burning love (electric fires, fur walls, bearskin rug, red hot tub, magic finger bed); and two erotic themes (bondage room and bordello). The romantic ideal is understandable and expected on a question of this type. People are seeking an escape from the everyday world. In fact, the ideas were somewhat inventive in the case of 'burning love' and 'in the clouds.'

The erotic suggestions are the most interesting. A female, 20, suggested a bondage room. She did not specify details. A male, 25, suggested a bordello theme; this notion seems to come directly from our culture. In reality, the hotel management discourages the "no-tell motel" theme and explicitly steers people away from that notion. The rooms originally encountered some opposition but people accepted the premise after a short time. According to one source, the hotel management is careful to avoid getting a bizarre reputation. Hotel staff discovered Polaroid film scraps in the Dungeon and asked the parties to leave (*Dallas Morning News*, May 5, 1987).

The last three themes were sports, recreational and transportation. Three people mentioned airplanes, two people specifying Lear jets and the Spirit of St. Louis, and one person mentioned a hot air balloon. According to a *New York Times* article (October 13, 1988), a Fantasuite hotel was seeking a jet fuselage for a prospective airplane Fantasy Suite. The recreational theme included the circus, a carnival and a motorcycle. These are very understandable and any item from this list seems potentially successful.

The last category, sports, featured four items. One person suggested a ski gondola and another a Swiss chalet. This is not surprising since area win-ters feature snow and much skiing. Two people suggested a theme room stressing wrestling. Both individuals mentioned that the bed could be shaped like a wrestling ring. The wrestling idea is appropriate considering the fantasy involved in selling the exhibitions through the media.

Several other general suggestions were included on the survey responses. One person suggested the presence of costumes and more interactive props in the room. For example, people could dress like an actor within that particular fantasy. According to the *Dallas Morning News* (1987), some people already dress up in the theme of the room: e.g., togas for Caesar's Courts, pith helmets for Jungle Safari or a steak dinner with the Wild West Fantasuite. The potential clearly exists for supplying these items if requested by hotel guests.

A second general suggestion was that Fantasy Suite patrons should have interaction with real persons. One survey respondent speculated on the possibility of a waitress on roller skates appearing in the Happy Days Cafe suite or sending a woman dressed as a belly dancer into the Arabian Nights suite for a brief appearance. This idea does have its merits and might prove successful if implemented in an appropriate manner.

Specific Complaints Recorded by Fantasuite Patrons

There were a number of complaints regarding the fantasy suite rooms. These complaints centered around hotel room upkeep, furnishings, and atmospheric factors. A male, 24, complained that the Dungeon had a bad television set and a hard bed. A second respondent, female, 25, complained that the Viking Room was not kept up, the bed was too short and there was no bubble bath. The comment that not enough towels were available in the room appeared on several occasions. A few people complained about smelling cigarette smoke in the Dungeon and several other rooms. In fact, room odors, whether caused by the humidifiers or bad upkeep were mentioned on a few occasions.

Furnishings were a popular category generating complaints. Some people complained of factors such as the small jacuzzi units in Happy Days Cafe and Cupid's Corner. One respondent complained that the Pearl Under the Sea needed more sea shells. Another person complained that the same room lacked enough seating area.

Complaints regarding atmospheric factors were particularly prominent. Three people mentioned that the mannequin behind the cashiers cage in the Gambler suite seemed intrusive. A female, 25, felt like she was being watched and suggested a retractable curtain. One respondent complained that Happy Days Cafe needed a jukebox and records from the 50s and 60s. Several people complained that their suites were not exotic enough. Complaints of this nature came from people staying in Arabian Nights and Eastern Winds. It should be noted that a single female, 20, stayed in Arabian Nights with her boyfriend and made this claim. Interestingly, she suggested the bondage suite as her choice of possible alternatives.

Other people complained of conditions such as that the television sets were not visible from bedroom settings, and the temperature in Igloo II and other suites were too warm. Two people complained that the suites were located in crowded public areas. They suggested that the intimate atmosphere desired in these suites was maximizable when outsiders from wedding parties and other organized business affairs were kept away from the Fantasuite area.

The Fantasuite concept is one form of a managed environment wherein the setting transcends the symbolic nature of the cultural setting in the structuring of human experience. Bourdieu (1984), Harvey (1989), and others might agree that the cultural views expressed in the surrounding are made accessible through specialized marketing and a planned economic strategy. Subsequent sections deal with the ultimate example of thematic environmental settings—Las Vegas, Disneyland and DisneyWorld.

LAS VEGAS AND TOURISM IN THE NEON JUNGLE

Las Vegas is the quintessential example of tourism from an experiential and social perspective. Benjamin "Bugsy" Siegel's original plan emphasized an isolated oasis offering escape from the real world. Las Vegas culture incorporated the consumption of every vice known to modern society. Consumers were afforded drinking, gambling, and sexual opportunities in a desert location.

Popular Hollywood movies play up the many surrealistic aspects of financial and social pressures experienced by Vegas tourists. *Honeymoon in Vegas* (1992) and *Indecent Proposal* (1993) play on the changing context offered by Las Vegas hotel operators. The gambling emphasis is placed on accumulating wealth and consuming the excitement of the gaming encounter. New gambling odds apply after every deal at the card table or dice throw at the craps table. Money continually changes hands in the interaction between casino employees and willing gamblers. Goffman (1971) published an important study on interaction in gambling situations. A chance conversation between a colleague and myself yielded the information that Goffman, shortly before his death, was researching the interaction between Atlantic City card dealers and table customers.

A discussion of Las Vegas assumes a relationship between economic and social aspects of everyday life. Las Vegas as a collective gambling enclave including a myriad number of individual hotel-casino complexes, provides entertainment and financial resources for maximum tourist enjoyment of their experience. Here the credit card is instrumental in charging airline tickets and hotel rooms.[23] Consumers can even obtain cash advances on their credit cards or instant gambling funds. The Vegas experience is predicated on the exchange of money for "chips"; or the conversion of currency into slot and video poker machine "credits" that are then utilized by the player.

Las Vegas is the perfect model of a postmodern location. First, the city offers a prototypical example of cultural capital. The entertainment and total ambience exploit tourist greed and a striving for excess as standard conditions of human nature. Tourists "consume" the scenery and symbolism as much as the alcohol, famous buffets, and gambling atmosphere. The total atmosphere represents staged authenticity.[24] The atmosphere may suggest an old Wild West scene (e.g., the cowboy neon sign in "Glitter Gulch"—a euphemism for downtown Vegas—and Binion's Horseshoe Casino hark back to a more primitive time). But the outside trappings are a mask for the economic motives behind the performance.

According to MacCannell (1989), the total surroundings are transformed into a social performance. Tourists express an interest in experiencing parasocial pleasure through attending Las Vegas stage shows and taking chances at blackjack tables, craps tables, and other games of chance. The live shows offer scantily clad women performing in world-renowned showrooms. Circus Maximus (Caesar's Palace), The Copa Room (Sands), now torn down and in renovation process, and The Flamingo Room (Flamingo) rank along with Radio City Music Hall and Disney World as several of the more respected entertainment centers.

The gambling atmosphere offers another "pseudo event" (or interaction for the purpose of generating economic revenue for the hotel operators). Visitors in Las Vegas must learn to look beyond the distraction created by obtrusive signs. MacCannell (1989) observes that experienced tourists learn how to read between the reality of a thriving Vegas gambling industry and the exterior signifiers. A visitor, seeing through the artificiality, wrote the following:

Along with winter vacationists, I will return to lively Las Vegas, if only to learn whether Howard Hughes, like the Mint Casino, has begun issuing free coupons entitling the visitor to a backstage tour of his moneymaking establishment (p. 127)

Second, Las Vegas emphasizes excess in providing a total immersion into an escapist environment. Each hotel casino puts on its best front to compete for visitors. The escapism includes an architectural view of large hotel-casino complexes; garish signs offering entertainment, food and gambling propositions; wedding chapels for "instant marriages"; and exterior attractions along the Vegas strip intended as tourist lures.

The architectural plans are unique and very distinctive. Each casino is designed around a particular theme. For example, Caesar's Palace emphasizes the Roman Empire, Circus Circus features actual circus acts, The Frontier maintains a western motif, Excalibur exemplifies a medieval look, and The Mirage consists of a South Seas setting. More particularly, Excalibur actually resembles a medieval fortress, while Circus Circus is derivative of a circus setting. The suggested themes are reinforced with dress uniforms worn by cocktail waitresses and dealers and uniquely designed or named sections of the casino or hotel areas.

The casino signs are also distinctive. Each major hotel casino located along the Las Vegas strip is promoted by a huge neon sign offering food specials, specific entertainment acts, and the best odds or sport book facilities. The huge sign outside Circus Circus features a giant clown billboarding the hotel's room accommodations and other information. The sign advertises the low-priced buffet specials, along with the usual gaming information.

Wedding chapels are a standard feature throughout the Vegas strip and within the major hotel casino complexes. Marriage ceremonies are available 24 hours a day. Some wedding chapels along the strip post signs indicating which celebrities were married in their facilities. Tourists often read in hometown newspapers how a particular celebrity (e.g., Earvin "Magic" Johnson or Warren Beatty) visited Las Vegas for a quickie wedding. Wedding chapels in a major hotel casino complex are postmodern examples of self-enclosed societies. In the case of a hotel such as Circus Circus or Imperial Palace, couples can get married and spend their honeymoon in the hotel without seeking outside entertainment. Food services, gambling, shopping, and other accommodations are available under one roof.

Additionally, the Las Vegas planners are extending the postmodern image planning among adults seeking sexual or gambling pleasure and family-oriented attractions incorporating children. Family entertainment is strongly emphasized as the Las Vegas casinos compete with local gambling operations across the country. Most notably, the Circus Circus corporation extended their specialization in family entertainment. They built a $300 million theme park "out of cash flow." The theme park is contained within a four-acre space frame. The structure incorporates a replica of the Grand Canyon, the largest roller coaster on the West Coast, a flume ride, and eight or nine dinosaurs (Arts and Entertainment Network, 1993).

Bill Kurtis, narrator of a television report on gambling, observes that the casinos offer fictional cartoon characters to children while providing gambling as escapism for adults:

You cannot see it immediately. The upfront colors are still as bright, and they carry the same old message. But behind the strobing neon it's a new game taken right from the Disney handbook. It's called family entertainment—and when you total up three or four days of hotel rooms, meals, arcade games for the kids—you have the mother lode of tourist dollars. (Arts and Entertainment Network, 1993)

The external architecture is equally important. Major competition for consumption of cultural capital through easy credit card access has created a need for drawing customers into the casinos.[25] In a manner not unlike the carnival barker promoting attractions inside the tent, hotels offer shows outside or surrounding their casino areas. The Mirage offers an example of staged authenticity with its recreation of a South Seas volcano. The volcano (powered by heated water and a highly pressured hydraulic system) "erupts" every 15 minutes from early evening until midnight. Massive crowds are drawn to the site. The volcano accompanies an interior exhibit featuring white tigers utilized by Siegfried and Roy in their famous illusion show, giant fish tanks behind the front desk, and a dolphin pool in the backyard.[26] This paragraph from a press release detailing the Mirage Resorts incorporated history describes the Mirage in a few sentences:

The Mirage is a tropically themed property which features a five acre front lagoon complete with a fire erupting volcano; a habitat for extremely rare Royal White Tigers as well as a habitat for six Atlantic Bottlenose Dolphins; a tropical rain forest with waterfalls and lagoons; and a 20,000 gallon salt water aquarium behind the front desk. (Mirage Hotel and Casino, 1993)

Caesar's Palace, which is located adjacent to The Mirage property, countered with its own version of staged authenticity. Caesar's had already established a unique identity through the transformation of the hotel casino into vestiges of the Roman Empire. Cleopatra's Barge is a bar contained in a replicated Nile barge. Local models dressed as Cleopatra, Julius Caesar and Marc Antony facilitate staged authenticity. The models mix with the crowd, pose for photographs, and act as unofficial greeters.

Caesar's reinforced its image with the addition of the Forum Mall. The mall, which opened in May 1992, consists of upscale shops serving to unite the early Roman theme with brisk tourist sales. Businesses operating under Roman-style storefronts include such famous names as Gucci, Victoria's Secret, Warner Brothers, Louis Vuitton, Spago, Nicky Blair's and Carnegie Deli. The mall is designed as an ancient Roman streetscape. Immense columns and arches, central piazzas, ornate fountains, and classical statues complete the effect. The ceiling emulates the Mediterranean sky, while several piazzas recreate ancient Rome.

In one piazza, a robotic statue of Bacchus, god of merriment and wine, is featured along with Apollo, Plutus, and Venus in a show featuring lasers, music and sound effects (Forum Mall, 1993). The Festival Fountain packs in hundreds of tourists during each hourly performance, featuring the robotic statues which actually move and speak. The performance draws potential gamblers into the mall. Additionally, tourists must leave the mall through the attached casino, where models dressed as Cleopatra and Caesar greet tourists at the casino entrance.[27]

Other hotels competed in a similar fashion. Steve Wynn, owner of the Golden Nugget and The Mirage, built a unique hotel-casino. Treasure Island is a hotel casino complementing The Mirage's Polynesian South Seas theme. A press release describing the new resort announced that operation's November 22, 1993 completion, four years after the opening of The Mirage. Steve Wynn is quoted as saying, "The sheer fun of it has virtually jumped off the pages of Robert Louis Stevenson's great novel and on to our blueprints" (Mirage Hotel and Casino, 1993).

The Circus Circus Corporation competed with its own version of staged authenticity. Luxur, a hotel casino, opened in 1993. The outside architecture is designed as a high-rise pyramid-shaped building. The theme features Queen Nefertiti and other aspects of ancient Egypt. The gambling special on the Arts and Entertainment cable station (Arts and Entertainment Network, 1993) highlighted plans for a two-performances-per-day Egyptian theme show, a Nile River ride through the casino, a state-of-the-art arcade, an Egyptian amusement park, a shopping mall, and other tourist attractions.

Each of these Las Vegas innovations is indicative of the postmodern theme wherein niche (or specialty marketing) is a recurrent theme. In effect, Las Vegas becomes an ersatz theme park driven by excited credit card—carrying tourists. The entire package begins with the exterior design and carries the detail through the entire interior down to the ash trays and drinking glasses, piped-in music, and employee uniforms. The experience is tied into creating cultural capital capable of attracting tourists into the casinos, shops, and restaurants.

The older downtown area offers its own version of Las Vegas glitz. The spectacular neon displays in the downtown "Glitter Gulch" area act as an extension of the strip area through exemplification of the overall garish atmosphere. The addition of a new mall-like atmosphere with nightly light shows enhances the appeal of this less attractive area. One might conclude that "all that glitters is not gold." The success of Las Vegas in the midst of several recessions and the allure of MGM's theme park tells us otherwise.

One is left to contemplate the postmodern phenomena created with initiating the competition for tourism—Disneyland and Disney World. The last major section in this chapter will analyze the two notable theme parks as seen through the creation of cultural capital.

"WE'RE GOING TO DISNEY WORLD!"

Perhaps the ultimate postmodern experience is found in an examination of Disneyland and Disney World. The Disney organization constructed idyllic theme park settings offering the prototypical tourist setting. Tourism and the purchase of souvenirs, lodging, and food are facilitated through the use of consumer credit. A family of four cannot easily afford $49 admission per person, overnight hotel lodgings, food, and other items without the use of credit cards.

Cultural capital and nostalgia are two important factors explaining the appeal of the Disney theme parks. The tourist attraction must offer a special appeal before travelers will spend their hard-earned money. Cultural capital is built into the appeal and image-making efforts of Disney Productions and subsequent byproducts. Featherstone (1991) explains that cultural capital is derived from economic and social values placed on experiences and intangible elements linked with social prestige.[28]

Disneyland and Disney World operate according to a similar principle. Cultural capital in the case of Disneyland and Disney World means that the environment transcends the economic value attached to admission, souvenirs, and other tourist expenditures. The frequent utilization of consumer credit enables the physical and emotional purchase of experience. The tourists are actively consuming and buying the ideal experience offered by the theme park. Image makers at the Disney theme parks work toward establishing a product with appeal for the average tourist. The product in question is a spotlessly clean, well-managed utopia wherein the problems of outside society are eradicated. The clockwork nature of the theme park environment and the staged authenticity of past, present, and future motifs compose a prototypical postmodern setting. Disneyland and Disney World are transformed into ersatz cities. A suspension of disbelief turns the idealized vision of society into a real experience in the mind of numerous tourists.

On a more universal level, Zukin (1991) views the architectural restructuring of inner-city areas (and, by extension, the idealization of theme parks as realms of power) as a postmodern reconstruction of "sociospatial relations by new patterns of investment which lead to counter-tendencies to urban decentralization through the redevelopment of inner city areas and docklands, which become gentrified by members of the new middle class and developed as sites of tourism and cultural consumption" (Featherstone, 1991, p. 107). In effect, the environment becomes museum-ified and equivalent to a theme park atmosphere.[29]

Interpersonal escape is one of the commodities purchased by consumers through utilization of credit devices. Featherstone underscores the point with a deliberate comparison between fairs and the experiences offered by department stores or other exhibitions:

The excitement and fears the fair can arouse is still captured today in films which highlight the way in which these liminal spaces are sites in which excitement, danger, and the shock of the grotesque merge with dreams and fantasies which threaten to overwhelm and engulf the spectators. Today fun fairs and theme parks such as Disneyland still retain this aspect, albeit in a more controlled de-control of the emotions, where adults are given permission to behave like children again. (p. 80)

The problem does not end with the idealization of experience permitting an exchange of economic transaction for cultural transaction. The task remains for the efficient construction of the staged authenticity. Popular appeal leads to a modernization of travel devices moving crowds from one area into another at Disneyland and Disney World. Ritzer (1993) analyzes how efficient theme parks are equated with McDonald's as organizations establishing rational procedures for controlling the flow of people. Drivers are directed toward the main gate of the park via a limited-range broadcast channel. Conveyor systems move visitors from one section of the park to another. Transportation is also an intricate part of many attractions (pp.51–52).

Rationalization, efficiency, and a staged authenticity capable of enhancing the cultural capital of the Disney theme parks constitute only one aspect of their appeal. Nostalgia, or a look toward the future, is another major reason for the success of these two major theme parks and their later spinoffs into resort areas, movie studios, and the Epcot Center. A tourist can visit Tom Sawyer's Island or the Main Street Cinema or explore projected advances in nuclear physics, space travel, and electronic devices. Featherstone (1991) most appropriately summed up the postmodern appeal of Disney World in a statement about postmodern cities as centers of consumption, play, and entertainment. The notion of the tourist gaze indicates that experiences visiting theme parks, shopping centers, malls, museums, and galleries are appropriate places for cultural consumption (pp. 101–102).

The relationship between the postmodern aspects of Disneyland and Disney World is further explained by Featherstone's reference to the relationship between consumption and leisure (a reflection of cultural capital) (p.103). Featherstone begins the section with a discussion of The West Edmonton Mall in Canada and the Metrocentre in England. He would no doubt add the Mall of America in Bloomington, Minnesota. Featherstone comments that the people become audiences moving through imagery designed to represent "sumptuousness and luxury" or to "summon up connotations of desirable exotic faraway places, and nostalgia for past emotional harmonies."[30]

Each of the sections is meant to invoke youthful feelings among adults bringing their children. Both Disneyland and Disney World are divided into distinct sectors. The various subthemes incorporated as separate sections include Tomorrowland, Fantasyland, Adventureland, Liberty Square, and Main Street. The attractions combine many theme rides (rocket ships, submarines, automobiles) and thrill rides (Space Mountain). In addition, Michael Jackson's 3D attraction Captain EO is offered at Disneyland and Disney World. Disneyland added Toonland, a section containing cartoon characters starring in *Who Framed Roger Rabbit?*

The Disney organization encapsulates a history of the Disney empire with extensive background detailed in their training manual.[31] Disneyland opened in 1955. The original Disneyland offered a connection between the past and hopes for the future. A regular Disney series on the television networks drew people to the theme park. Walt Disney expanded the reach of his theme park with several attractions at the 1964 World's Fair in New York. "Great Moments with Mr. Lincoln" (a truly postmodern spectacle where an electronic robot replicated Abraham Lincoln's notable speeches) and "It's a Small World After All" were two of the famous attractions offered at the fair. Both attractions are staples at Disneyland and Disney World.

Major planning for Disney World started in the mid 1960s. Disney World was a portion of an extensive Walt Disney World Resort. The facility opened on October 1, 1971. Some early features of the development included the Magic Kingdom, the Contemporary Resort Hotel, and the Polynesian Resort. Space Mountain, the Disney Inn, Walt Disney World Village, Typhoon Lagoon, Pleasure Island, Disney Village Marketplace, and numerous resort areas followed.

Epcot Center opened in 1982. The theme park is a showcase for new technologies and cultures of man. Epcot Center emphasized the relationship between humans and the environment. The Epcot resort area included a Yacht and Beach Resort, the Walt Disney World Dolphin, the Walt Disney World Swan, and Disney's Caribbean Beach Resort.

More recently, the Disney organization has built theme parks in Japan (Tokyo Disneyland) and Paris, France (EuroDisney). Both theme parks charge higher admission charges than their American counterparts but are immensely successful.

The Disney-MGM Studios Theme Park was added several years ago. The area includes an active movie studio modeled after the long-standing Universal Studio attraction in southern California. Many television shows are also produced in the theme park. The theme park features many movie- and television-related rides (e.g., Indiana Jones Stunt Show, Beauty and the Beast, a Star Wars Thrill Ride, and Teenage Mutant Ninja Turtles). The theme park also features a Superstar Television exhibit. In a real postmodern twist, visitors are electronically juxtaposed with videotape from

The Today Show, Golden Girls, General Hospital, Howdy Doody and *The Tonight Show*.

How do we explain the postmodern appeal of a Disney theme park and related economic implications? Aside from the previously discussed concept of experience drawing on and creating cultural capital, the theme parks continually play on childhood nostalgia and the "little boy or girl in all of us." Zukin (1991) and other urban sociologists emphasize the development of theme parks into idyllic microcosmic cities. The Disney organization training manual amplifies Disney World's considerable symbolic (or cultural) success in stating that Walt Disney World Resort is more than a theme park. According to the text, "It is a worldwide legend" (Walt Disney Organization, 1993, p. 4). The manual summarizes all of the postmodern attractions contributing to its popular tourist acceptance and economic success.[32]

The Disney World marketing plan reflects the tradition of postmodern segmentation. Niche marketing is operative in the process. Each individual group has its own predispositions which must be analyzed and defined according to Disney's own marketing calculations. Discrete consumer categories are created and defined according to individual groups of people "each of which must be talked to in a different way" (pp. 1–3). The specific groups are national, in-state, family, nonfamily, new markets, and international. The consumer groups, all of which are categorizable according to discernible characteristics, are approached according to family size, travel distance, and monetary cost managed through credit card expenditures.

The message itself is a product of astute promotional efforts. A "campaign" recognizable throughout the marketplace is constructed for the general media campaign. The marketing section within the training manual specifically mentions the 1981 campaign celebrating the World Disney World Tencennial; the 1982 opening of the Epcot Center; the 1986 fifteenth anniversary party featuring a prize given to a guest every 15 seconds and a new car given away every day, all year long; and the 1988 theme highlighting the sixtieth birthday of Mickey Mouse.

The so-called marketing mosaic is based on publicity derived from anything seen or heard in the news media (newspapers, magazines, television, and radio). The marketing, in a version of the gatekeeper process, involves news releases and photographs packed into press kits and sent to newspapers around the country. Video press kits incorporating completed video stories are distributed to TV reporters. Press tours feature local meetings with Walt Disney World representatives in cities throughout the country. Satellite hookups make press events available to media throughout the country.

Advertising is specifically directed into television, print advertising, and onsight advertising. The various segments discussed in previous segments are isolated, targeted, and approached on the basis of the following strategy:

Television is the most powerful means of advertising to many market segments because the visual nature of TV allows us to show our very visual product. A picture is worth ten thousand words when we show the smile on a youngster's face, or the bright blue water and snow-white sand of a beach scene. (Walt Disney Organization, 1993, p. 19)

The Disney World marketing scheme stemmed from the original vision for Disneyland as posed by the Disney Corporation. According to Zukin (1991), Disneyland's original critics "failed to understand that Disneyland was an ideal object for visual consumption, a landscape of social power" (p. 223). In effect, Disneyland projected "a 'Disneyland realism,' sort of Utopian in nature, where we [Disneyland's planners] carefully program out all the negative, unwanted elements and program in the positive elements" (p. 222).

Disneyland and Disney World are designated as unique tourist attractions. The theme parks constitute "fantasy architecture for mass entertainment" (p. 232). The collective desires of the mass society were incorporated into the planning for specific themes appealing to tourist interests. Mass consumption, in a manner not unlike the previous forms of cultural capital discussed in this chapter, was facilitated through the symbolic settings (or liminality—otherwise known as barriers—set by the physical background and nostalgia or yearning for utopian society).

The Disney theme parks are also important as they impact market, place, and landscape.[33] Zukin (1991) forcefully argues that market culture is determined by place (p. 1). Settings dictate existing culture. Place eventually has become less important with the homogenization of American society. Experiences lack individual creativity with the imposition of global cultures. Landscape is the symbolic representation of cultural values. The landscaped setting is trivialized as an archetype consumable just like physical objects purchased by zealous shoppers.

In effect, tourism facilitated through credit card utilization brings corporate control into consumer consumption of social leisure. We are told what to see, we are programmed into reacting in a particular fashion while consuming sexual fantasy or visions of winning money in the Las Vegas-induced theme park landscape; and we are convinced that a consultation with a telephone psychic will change our lives. All of these above are a form of social escape. However, consumer conception of social escape does not instantly materialize through natural experience. The next chapter offers a deconstruction of credit card advertising images used in communicating aesthetic values.

NOTES

1. Schor (1991) notes the conspicuously high standard of living enjoyed by American Families in the following passage:

After four decades of this shopping spree, the American Standard of living embodies a level of material comfort unprecedented in human history. The American home is more spacious and luxurious then the dwellings of any other nation. Food is cheap and abundant. The typical family owns a fantastic array of household and consumer appliances: we have machines to wash our clothes and dishes, mow our lawns, and blow away our snow. On a per person basis, yearly income is nearly $22,000 a year—or sixty five times the average income of half the world's population. (p. 3)

2. A later section of this dissertation study will expand on Zukin (1991) in dealing with Disneyland/Disney World as distinct cultural manifestations.

3. "The Club" (a device intended to thwart automobile theft by snapping onto the steering wheel) was successful because the former clutch-locking system was impractical with the driver's side relocation of the automatic transmission. Manufacturers of the anti theft device found themselves competing against imitation products. Therefore, they sought to redefine the original product through introduction of the same device in various colors. A currently running television commercial subtly points out the reconstructed product image.

4. Analysis of shared symbols and symbolic interaction as applied to the foregoing analysis is largely derived from Thorstein Veblen's *Theory of the Leisure Class*, 1899/1967 and Erving Goffman's *Presentation of Self in Everyday Life*, 1959. MacCannell's (1989) analysis of the tourist draws heavily from the collective work of both authors.

5. MacCannell utilizes the term in a generic context in offering a semiotic analysis of everyday experience.

6. The talk radio format combined the telephone with broadcast radio conversation. Anonymity of personal identity often enables the expression of private thoughts without public attrition. Goffman (1959) dissects this concern is his discussion of "discredited" and "discreditable."

7. Sexual attractiveness plays a vital role in the process. Most messages are straightforward, with the occasional exception of double entendre enticement. One such example was overheard in April 1984: Hi there. I'm bachelorette number X. Do you want to play a game? If you win, you get me. You must be intelligent, attractive, and have a fabulous sense of humor. You must be dynamic and very successful. Do you like older women? I like younger men. So if you are about six feet tall and have a great body, I want to hear from you. You just might be the winner. Please send me your picture along with your letter. Maybe when you are the lucky winner, you'll find out that you have a lucky prize. I hope to hear from you soon. That's bachelorette X.

8. Sexual tensions are handled differently in various situations. Examples illustrate compatible and tenuous situations.

Driver: Hi, [Handle].
Prostitute: Hi, [inaudible].
Driver: This here's [Handle].
You all wanna have coffee wit' me?
Prostitute: Yeh, I [inaudible].
Driver: Yeh, Okay.
I'm just poking along 40 MPH up here. Ah, come on.
Prostitute: [inaudible]—55.
Driver: Fine. Ah-you wanna stop at this ah-what is it-a Skelly up here at the right hand side?
Driver: Yeh-ah-okay-what are you drivin'?
(Klein and Luxenburg, 1981:12).

Driver: Where's that horny woman at? How much would it take to satisfy you?
Prostitute: About 12 inches and $25. Come in.
Driver: I got the 12 inches, but I don't have $25.

9. A comment filed with the Federal Communications Commission by Morality in Media, Inc. (1984) explains this system. The Downstate Mass Announcement Network Service (known as "Dial-it" numbers) was leased by New York Telephone to private business sponsors. This service uses a special switching system that permits one number to handle thousands of calls simultaneously.

10. Refer to Steve Richard's description of an adult bookstore as presented at the 1983 meeting of the Society for the Study of Social Problems in Detroit, Michigan (See Richard, 1983).

11. Three recorded Dial a Porn segments suggesting a panties fetish, rectal sex, and fellatio and a fourth suggesting penis stimulation (the last cited by Morality in Media, Inc.) were overheard on the phone line.

12. The Psychic Friends Service Network and various competitors generally offer personal advice for a set rate per minute. The payment is generally billed on a credit card.

13. The structural framework of the psychic hotlines were discussed on a February 1993 edition of *The Maury Povich Show* (Povich, 1993).

14. Everyday culture is inundated with sexual images. Most television programs (soap operas, television talk programs, and even the news programs) television commercials, magazine advertising, and daily discourse emphasize sexual imagery.

15. More recently, the viable interpretation shifts frim the Marxist Paradigm to a less deterministic explanation. The postmodern (or poststructural) view assumes that consumers pursue experiences or commodities as a matter of free will rather than manipulation. Of course, marketing still plays a major part in the decision making process. But consumers still pick and choose among offered material or experiential options.

16. Ford could not recognize that the advent of modern industrial changes stemming from his creation possessed the potential for effecting impressive change in the form of industrial planning and production.

17. These fantasy suites offer luxuries generally unavailable at home. Utilization of consumer credit enables the njoymentof the following fantacies (pamphlet descriptions include the following details):

- *Infinity.* A predominance of lights and mirrors. The room contains a queen-size bed with a stereo and cassette player built into the headboard. A jacuzzi is included in this fantasy suite.

- *Captain's Quarters.* A paneled cabin included a porthole. The room is equipped with a waterbed and jacuzzi.

- *Eastern Winds.* A king-size bed, black lacquered furniture, and oriental decor are included along with a jacuzzi, ceiling-to-floor mirrors, and jets of water.

- *Cupid's Corner.* The room contains a heart-shaped waterbed, mirrored ceiling, stereo, and cassette player.

- *Space Odyssey.* Guests sleep in a recreation of a Gemini space capsule set in a moonscape. This waterbed capsule includes an AM/FM stereo cassette player, TV, and videogame player. A jacuzzi is also included.

- *LeCave.* A waterbed and oversized tub are featured in a cavelike setting.

18. Several other suites complete the set of 24 formerly offered at the West Bend Fantasy Suite Hotel. These include the following themes:

- *Pearl Under the Sea.* Clam shell waterbed; lighting controls and AM/FM stereo cassette player; private tub surrounded by mirrors.

- *Viking.* Viking ship with waterbed; private spa; sauna.

- *The Treehouse.* Swinging bed suspended from four trees; jacuzzi.

- *Jungle Safari.* Grass hut with waterbed and TV; whirlpool.

- *The Dungeon.* Medieval castle enhanced with a giant jacuzzi.

- *The Tepee.* Tepee equipped with a waterbed and mirrored ceiling; large jacuzzi amid a forest setting.

- *Tijuana Jail.* Jail cell furnished with a queen-size bed; large jacuzzi.

- *The Gambler.* Wall mural of Atlantic City; furnished in red and black; queen-size bed with mirrored and lighted headboard; walk up jacuzzi, surrounded by mirrors; woman behind cashier's counter; gambling equipment.

- *Klondike.* Queen size mining cart; TV; bath.

- *Happy Days Cafe.* Giant jacuzzi cup and coffee urn; queen-size sandwich bed; fifties cafe setting.

- *Wild, Wild West.* Wagon train bed; water trough jacuzzi.

- *Arabian Nights.* Sheik's tent, ten-sided waterbed; oriental rug.

- *Baby Grand.* Waterbed in a piano.

- *Pharaoh's Tomb.* Sarcophagus bed in a pyramid; tub cornered by mirrors and hieroglyphics.

19. The marketing director at the West Bend FantasySuite Hotel answered questions regarding hotel clientele, attitudes of the hotel chain management toward the Fantasuite program, and public receptiveness to the Fantasuite concept.

20. These results reflect the upwardly mobile nature of the American public. Males have already worked at achieving graduate degrees, while females are increasingly pursuing a college education and gradually positioning themselves toward graduate degree programs. The predominantly younger females in this survey, mostly in their mid twenties, reflect this growing trend.

21. We could not document exactly how many males or females were married but engage in extramarital relationships.

22. Several factors bear clarification. The Fantasuites were featured on *Lifestyles of the Rich and Famous*, in numerous newspaper articles (*New York Times*, 1988; *Chicago Tribune*, 1986; *Dallas Morning News*, 1987), and on a local radio station. The hotel made six suites available as a radio station promotion. The guests stayed on a weekday night and were part of a live broadcast the following morning. The suites involved in the promotion were Caesar's Court, Happy Days Cafe, Pharaoh's Tomb, Viking, Gambler, and LeCave.

23. An academician encountered at a sociology conference confessed that she accepted her only credit card after hotels, airlines and car rental firms refused cash payment.

24. MacCannell (1989) discusses the tourist appeal within settings wherein the immediate background consists of actors and actresses portraying historical roles. Relevant examples of staged authenticity include the re-creation of colonial life in Williamsburg, the construction of antiquated villages throughout Long Island, New York, and the bucolic (or rustic) Main Street, USA attractions throughout the country.

25. Recurrent reports indicate that some slot machines may accept credit cards or plastic cards simulating the easy access or cash through ATM cards. It is noteworthy that most casinos in Las Vegas and Atlantic City include either ATM machines or cash call devices wherein gamblers can obtain instant cash.

26. These attractions were amply illustrated in *Gambling in America*, an Investigative Reports production on the Arts and Entertainment (A&E) cable television, April 9, 1993.

27. Bill Kurtis, narrator of the A&E report on gambling, pointed out that casinos are transformed into theme parks. This observation is especially relevant in the case of *Circus Circus*, where parents and children can spend a minimum of $2000 for a short two-day vacation. The total includes credit card purchases of airline tickets, hotel accommodations, extra cash, food, and souvenirs.

28. Featherstone (1991, p. 89) elaborated on this important point. He indicated that discussion of lifestyles and cultural goods included volume and economic capital. Featherstone's important point about cultural capital indicates that the cultural realm has its own "logic and currency" as well as economic capital.

29. Featherstone (1991:106) offers the following justification for this view surrounding cultural capital:

From economic utility of cultural capital this means that while traditional smokestack industrial towns of the "rust belt" are to be regarded as low in cultural capital (with the exception of those who are able to repackage and museumify these elements as assets), the range is extended from traditional historic value and treasures to include newly created and simulated environments that take in some of the postmodern and more popular cultural forms we have mentioned (theme parks, malls, shopping centres, museums as well as popular cultural venues), which are perceived as attractive and saleable. (p. 106)

30. Some of Featherstone's description covered the deindustrialization of cities and the expansion of shopping centers. The common themes or messages between the shopping centers, mall, museums, theme parks, and tourist experiences are a form of cultural consumption.

31. The material was obtained in February 1992 after contacting Disney representatives.

32. These features include the scope of tourist activity, profitability, and modern communications features.

33. Zukin's primary framework in *Landscapes of Power: From Detroit to Disney-World* (1991).

4

The Advertising Industry

The advertising industry assumes an important function in promoting the purchase of various commodities. The existence and utility of various salable products or services are publicized through various media. Television advertising features promotional commercials ranging in length from 10 to 60 seconds. Newspaper and magazine print formats, radio commercials, highway billboards, and even matchbook covers are other popular advertising forms.

The analysis presented in this section focuses on the creation of consumer credit marketing concepts and how messages are structured in television, radio, and magazine advertising. Does the advertising industry alter public attitudes? The overall analysis facilitates an evaluation of whether the consumer credit industry "seduces the masses" or essentially plays on predispositions already present among many societal members. The analysis also undertakes a consideration of whether a combination of these factors are operative.

The cumulative analysis isolates several important historical factors for consideration. These factors include proliferation of mass media in the form of television, magazines, and other communications technology; increased establishment of nuclear families in the post–World War II era; and growing sophistication of advertising techniques as a major influence in the basic process.

Each media form is instrumental in publicizing consumer credit. Conspicuous advertising in various media promotes the social benefits of using credit cards. Credit card advertising is so prominent because virtually every person is exposed to mass media. Some forms include television, magazines, and newspapers. Television penetrates over 90 percent of all American homes. In addition, magazines and newspapers reach many persons and are heavily dependent on advertising revenue. The relative advantage of magazines and newspapers is the potential for repeated exposure of advertising copy among many people.

The nuclear family was a conspicuous social unit in the decades following World War II. Consumer demand rose in relation to family needs and media exposure. Television and other media expanded into all facets of social life. The rise of television and conspicuous sponsorship by leading manufacturers is directly linked with the new family lifestyle. It is not coincidental that television and other mass circulation media were prominently influential in publicizing and expanding consumer credit.

Finally, consumer credit was also marketed as an everyday product. Advertising messages evolved into a more subtle and sophisticated art form. Advertising was aimed at particular target audiences. Each campaign had a specific purpose and was organized around selling particular products. The emphasis on selling previously unavailable durable goods or experiences or merely altering the marketing image for greater sales is a prime function of advertising. Niche marketing is accomplished through carefully constructed commercials designed for informing public segments with potential interest in the goods and services. The public receives the message that credit cards can facilitate the purchase of particular goods and services.

RATIONALIZATION WITHIN THE ADVERTISING INDUSTRY

Advertising fulfills an important purpose within a capitalist society. Actual merchandise and credit cards (as purchasing devices) are vigorously marketed in a competitive capitalist economy. The evolution of credit instruments for financing current and prospective purchases is equated with marketing specific merchandise. At the same time, there is an essential difference between selling particular consumer goods and promoting the future acquisition of those commodities through credit card privileges.

Marketing the potential consumer purchase of material items or experiences such as trips to Las Vegas, the Mall of America, or Disney World is more important than the immediate sale of a refrigerator or videocassette recorder. Future consumption is an important consideration, given that Sears issued 41.2 million Discover Cards; Citibank issued 30 million MasterCards and Visa cards, and American Express issued 25 million cards by the mid-1980s. The current balance on credit cards averages about $1,260 for Visa, MasterCard, Discover, and Optima Cards. The outstanding balance average was only $800 in 1986. There are a total number of 275 million credit cards in circulation, up from the 180 million in 1986 (Mandell, 1990). According to market share, there is an industry total of $189 billion in outstanding balances. The major card issuers rank as follows: Citicorp, $34 billion, 18 percent; Sears Discover, $14.9 billion, 7.9 percent; Chase Manhattan, $10.0 billion, 5.3 percent; Bank of America, $9.6 billion, 5.1 percent; MBNA America, $8.3 billion, 4.4 percent; First Chicago, $7.4 billion, 3.9 percent; Chemical Bank, $6.0 billion, 3.2 percent; AT&T Universal, $5.2 billion, 2.8 percent, Banc One, $4.6 billion, 2.4 percent; and Household Bank, $4.3 billion, 2.3 percent (Bryant, 1992).

Credit cards, as promoted by banks, finance lending companies, and home equity loans, a vigorously marketed consumer line of credit popular within periods of low interest rates, enabled the purchase of other consumer commodities. Additionally, retailing outlets depend on credit cards and installment plans for approximately half of their overall sales volume (National Retail Merchants Association, 1986).

Not everyone shares the same instrumental view regarding the positive impact of consumer credit. O'Connor (1982) infers that advertising is a manipulative force responsible for commodity accumulation. Wants become transformed into needs as advertising artificially imposes influences redirecting the focus of consumer purchasing decisions. The economy is adversely affected in the shift from directed savings to deliberate consumption. An analysis of seminal work by Leiss et al. (1984); Jhally and Leiss (1986); and Jhally (1987) completes the link between O'Connor's general thesis and the critical analysis of advertising and its impact.[1]

The advantages of consumer commodity acquisition are stressed in the formulation of an effective advertising campaign. Advertisers and creative copywriters are emphasizing the fulfillment of corporately designated wants and needs, as informed by marketing research and epitomized in consumption activity (Leiss, 1976). Leiss detailed how advertising and culture are linked in the satisfaction of needs. A "psychology of scarcity" is associated with social interaction wherein

individuals encourage each other to believe that failure to procure the means for purchasing certain goods will exclude them from all hope of satisfying the needs which have come to be associated with these goods. (Leiss, 1976, p. 31)

Other affluent or "pseudo-affluent" members of the population follow these trendsetters, in the manner of "keeping up with the Joneses," but at great financial peril. Bankruptcy is a distinct possibility when consumers conspicuously "buy" into these ideologies and support their desires with borrowed money. The inevitable result is elimination from the system through cutoff of these credit resources.

Advertisers are immediately less concerned with the bankruptcy problem than with creating or channeling into consumer demand. The process by which these advertisement placement decisions are made and the nature of the message explains this last point. The marketing concept, depiction of the message and the eventual reception of the product by the American consumer are three vital parts of the process. These elements are common in organized campaigns highlighting the desirability of particular products. Analysis of each component is present within subsequent sections of this chapter on consumer credit advertising.

There are noteworthy issues associated with any analysis of the advertising industry and its impact on consumer behavior. These factors include marketing of actual produced commodities or credit instruments for the purchase of goods; how advertising projects particular themes; the emotional level of commodity or credit instrument advertising; and the targets or particular audience segments selected by advertisers and creative advertising agency efforts. An examination of consumer credit advertising presented in this section emphasizes the differences between selling tangible material items such as automobiles or nebulous multipurpose instruments that include credit cards, loans and second mortgages. The appeal of each item is structured differently within carefully created advertising campaigns. Each advertised product has certain common features (such as sales pitch, upbeat message, and story line).

Additionally, the art of advertising has influenced television audience perception and marketing strategies employed by financial institutions. Advertising images created through specifically focused advertising campaigns alter the expansion of services offered by finance companies, banks, and credit card companies. Consumer receptivity to credit offered by these institutions encourages additional programs aimed at enhancing already existing services (buyer protection plans, lemon protection laws, price protection plans).

At the same time, consumer decisions create new incentives for the diversification of the consumer credit industry. This analysis will focus upon creation of specific marketing concepts and how the message is structured in advertisements shown on television and contained in magazine copy. A consideration of how consumers interpret the message is a larger question left for a future study.

Consumer credit, in the form of credit cards, automobile loans and finance and home equity loans, has become a staple in the lifestyles of average Americans. Aggregate consumer credit volume has increased from several million dollars in the early 1960s to $2 trillion in 1987. This financial figure does not include mortgage loans, which are counted as long-term debt rather than installment credit (Federal Reserve Board, 1988). Additionally, disposable personal income for all Americans was $3.2 billion in 1987 and $13,157 per capita (U.S. Bureau of the Census, 1987).

Americans now had more discretionary income at their disposal in the form of higher salaries derived from professional duties and banking lines of credit. Advertisers tapped into this potential group of willing consumers. Advertising campaigns channeled this spending power into commodities and services promoted by the business sector. Consumer products were actively marketed as commodities that people could buy through purposeful allocation of this enhanced spending power.

The formulation and promotion of advertising campaigns became the responsibility of designated professional agencies. These agencies worked with commercial clients in structuring a public image capable of encouraging increased consumer business. Bensman (1971) pointed out that these advertising agencies operated along bureaucratic and ethical considerations in producing potentially successful advertising campaigns. The resulting campaigns were carefully prepared by teams of professionals working on every aspect of the public relations image: from conceptualization of the original design through consumer research, artist depictions, and final print or filmed displays.

Advertising can serve at least two roles: it can create new consumer wants capable of conversion into consumer needs or sustain a preexisting consumer predisposition. These two roles are represented in the critiques presented by Stuart Ewen (1976, 1988); Ewen and Ewen (1983); and Michael Schudson (1984). Ewen claimed that advertising was an integral mechanism in the emerging consumer society that initially developed in the 1920s and continues through the present time. Advertising played an important role in presenting the American public with new social values oriented toward creating and sustaining consumer behavior.

According to Ewen's argument, capitalist culture depended upon advertising as a vehicle for selling previously nonexistent ideology and lifestyles. Ewen utilized the concept "Captains of Consciousness" in signifying the presentation of ideological assumptions through advertising. A new way of life was projected through the efforts of advertising agencies. Advertising regularly depicted the male as the "breadwinner," and the women and children as dependent on commodities made affordable through the efforts of the male role of "wage slave." Thus, Ewen would perceive advertising as a prime motivator of increased consumption.

The rationality of the advertising process is based on either an attempted restructuring of expected consumer behavior or taking consumer predispositions and encouraging particular purchasing decisions. Ewen (1976) believes in the former: that much of the final advertising product promotes altered perceptions ultimately guiding or manipulating consumer spending choices.

Restructured gender roles are one such example. Women were portrayed as traditional housewives in produced advertising content prior to the 1960s. McGovern (1987) demonstrated how advertising from the early 1900s through 1945 depicted females as happy housewives. Women were placed in the kitchen or cast within maternal roles.

Gitlin (1983) concurs with this view. In his discussion of prime time ideology, he notes how this image underwent transformation into the woman's liberation model. Women had minds of their own and could finally struggle in the workplace along with the hard-pressed male population. Advertising executives seized upon the family unit as the major social force behind consumer purchasing activity. Social role expectations were carefully structured in marketing particular products among targeted audiences. For example, women of the 1920s were presented with the following image:

In the middle of her mechanically engineered kitchen, the modern housewife was expected to be overcome with the issue of whether her "self," her body, her personality were viable in the sociosexual market that defined her job.... A booklet advertising feminine beauty aids had on its cover a picture of a highly scrubbed, powdered and decorated nude. The message of the title was explicit: "Your Masterpiece=Yourself." Women were being educated to look at themselves as things to be created competitively against other women: painted and sculpted with the aids of the modern market. (Ewen, 1976, p. 197–208)

Marcuse (1964) was influential in framing these and related ideas. Marcuse claimed that these images reflected the formation of false consciousness. Woman's self-image was the culmination of results created through owning or using a product. Beauty aids or cosmetics are one such example. In 1986, the beauty industry sold women over $4 billion in perfume and cosmetics. The male grooming market approximated $1.3 billion during that same year (Donahue, 1988).

Ewen also examined the institutions responsible for promoting a highly visible consumer identification with commodities. Ewen's discussion of the social historical impact of these media developments includes an interesting observation on the effect of game shows offering merchandise as promotional vehicles. The original *The Price Is Right*, not the revival initiated during the 1970s, was a reflection of these trends:

Quiz shows, common fare during the 1950s, produced an imagery of abundance and the easy accessibility of goods. On shows, like the Goodson-Todman production of The Price is Right, the audience was not only treated to a parade of the wares of the marketplace but was vicariously rewarded for internalizing a blend of dependent infantilism and a correct sense of the actual retail prices ("Without going over") of products. Indeed, the tag prices of all kinds of goods had become useful knowledge in a world in which these items were flooding market counters and being touted and screamed over by modern housewives on the TV giveaways. (Ewen, 1976, p. 209)

Television game shows have always spearheaded the display of consumer goods as a desirable social image. Many television game shows featured a quest for valued merchandise. Specific programs during the last 20 years included *Sale of the Century* (where contestants accumulated points used for purchasing consumer goods), the original *Wheel of Fortune* (contestants selected merchandise in exchange for accumulated points), and a Home Shopping game show promising the combination of studio contestants winning prizes and an opportunity for home viewers to purchase the same merchandise.

These programs promote automobiles, vacations, furniture and other consumer commodities. Permeations of consumer commodity orientations are reflected on these programs. A viewer watching *The Price Is Right* notices that the audience internalizes the prices of automobiles and other merchandise. They will shout out prices when on-stage contestants are competing for prizes. *Wheel of Fortune* once featured a version of this format. Contestants solved the puzzles with hopes of buying merchandise with winnings from each round and advancing toward the bonus round. New automobiles or other expensive items were offered. Emphasis is now placed on accumulating cash. The eventual winner can solve a bonus puzzle and win very expensive merchandise.

One might note that this program also marketed the selling of a major media personality. The meteoric career of Vanna White, a television model and letter turner on *Wheel of Fortune* embodies this worship. The appeal is enhanced with the accommodation of Vanna White's physical appearance. An ongoing promotional campaign once used the slogan "What will Vanna wear tonight?" In fact, a more recent advertising campaign further transformed Vanna White into a commodity with "The Wheel turns. Vanna turns." The commercial presented several examples of Vanna doing her fashion turn in a backless evening gown. Vanna has become an icon by virtue of her skillful handling of merchandise, prosocial encouragement of contestant aspirations, and the relentless publicity about her.

There is an alternative view on this issue. Schudson (1984) notes that advertising created through the collective efforts of corporate teams may not have an instant effect. He emphasizes that advertising is "an uneasy persuasion." Schudson's essential thesis is that advertising agencies make educated guesses and cannot predict the impact of an advertising campaign until its success or failure becomes apparent.

Proponents of this perspective downplay the Svengali-like properties associated with advertising. They often claim that people will not accept imposed value choices. A similar observation was also expressed by a highly placed advertising executive contacted in the formative stages of this report (personal interview, 1983). This individual, former account executive for MasterCard at the William Esty Advertising Agency, expressed the view that advertising does not always work as originally planned. Some campaigns fail when unforeseen viewer perceptions are reflected in consumer nonacceptance of the product.

Schudson notes that there is a science within the process of selling credit cards (or, as we add here, any form of consumer credit). Advertising agencies sample consumer demand through focus groups (interviewed consumer samples), testing completed commercials through storyboard research analysis, and commissioned studies through consumer research organizations.

Educated research is only one step in the process. Schudson has also noted that prior success breeds future success (personal conversation, 1984). One good advertising campaign produced others as reinforcers of the earlier efforts. Some examples of this are discussed later in this chapter. Not only was advertising reinforcing previously existent consumer attitudes, but good advertising was followed by more potent campaigns capitalizing on successes (as in movie sequels like *Terminator II* that reinforce earlier box office smashes).

Schudson employs a criticism of institutional practices rather than undertaking the socio-historical analysis employed by Ewen. A strength of Schudson's analysis is shown in an analysis of how credit cards were repositioned for a new consumer market. Women were courted by credit card companies with the advent of the drive for equal economic status. American Express actively recruited women.[2] The other major bank credit cards followed shortly thereafter. The strategy worked because women started using their financial "clout" gained through more active participation in the workforce.

Increased consumer acceptance of credit cards throughout the 1970s was an indication of good advertising campaigns. The advertising campaigns prepared by agencies representing MasterCard, Visa, and American Express focused on the changing social roles of men and women. Women were now middle aged college students, attractive models exuding symbolic economic power, or professionals accompanied by male friends and engaged in "breaking in" a new credit card.

Schudson's point of view carries more credibility than Ewen's argument about the manipulative power of advertising. The American public is not easily influenced by messages running counter to their own personal beliefs. In effect, Schudson's dismissal of the deterministic aspects of media runs counter to the often-stated claim that the media engage in agenda setting (or modification of consumer beliefs).[3] I believe that Schudson's view seems more credible. The agenda setting perspective can account for some change in public attitudes attributable to media influence. However, the mass media is only one factor in a set of other socializing forces comprising family background, occupational status, and religious influence.

In sum, Schudson and other advertising executives firmly believe that each consumer credit campaign incorporates a rationality accounting for consumer credit acceptance. Motivation stimulated by already predisposed attitudes prompts consumer desire for a particular credit card or installment financing. The nature of these cultural predispositions and the actual advertising process follows in succeeding sections.

CULTURAL INFLUENCE OF CONSUMER CREDIT

Consumer credit is solidly based within a wider societal context. An understanding of various advertising campaigns is dependent on recognizing how consumer credit has transcended a consumer convenience and become essential in everyday lifestyles.

People measure their status according to the numbers of types of cards owned. In 1982, Randall Collins indicated that America had become a "credentialed society" with status attainment dependent on educational achievement. This status benchmark is exploited for economic profit by the financial industry. An ordinary American Express card, MasterCard, or Visa was once a prized possession among many upper-middle, and middle class professionals. All that has changed with modern advertising campaigns.

The stakes have been raised with the active marketing of the American Express Gold Card, Gold MasterCard, and Gold Visa Card. These "golden opportunities" offer a higher credit line and more conveniences synonymous with business needs. Additionally, the various gold cards offer 90-day product protection for commodities purchased with those financial instruments, facilitated car rentals with automatic liability and personal accident coverage, and guaranteed ticket reservations for specially designated events (as initiated by the American Express Company).

Some credit advantages are still left reserved for the more economically advantaged. More impetus for rewarding business productivity was provided by the American Express Platinum Card. The platinum card carries an even higher credit line and is underwritten by participating banks.

American Express advertises the platinum card in upscale business magazines. The relatively limited marketability of this credit instrument does not warrant allocating (or targeting) some portion of the advertising budget toward mass marketing in the general media.

This information is important because we can see how the credit card industry is continually emphasizing the need for new financial products. A gold card was once perceived as a product reserved for the relatively affluent. But the shifting cultural values prompted by the ever-expanding credentialed society have resulted in a democratization of a formerly limited product. Professional and college football games regularly feature commercials emphasizing how the average person can benefit from credit card features. These features were previously marketed expressly for businessmen in higher-income categories.

A Gold MasterCard commercial presents a jigsaw puzzle completed with symbols representing flexible airline ticketing, enhanced credit lines, buyer protection, and other services. American Express has competing advertisements that stress the yearly financial activity statement provided to the gold card customers. The service is noteworthy because consumers can still deduct a small percentage of their installment payments and professional expenses on their current income tax forms.

MasterCard, Visa, American Express, and Sears (the Discover card) are four major marketing organizations engaged in the distribution and promotion of widely held credit cards. Visa, MasterCard and American Express have been in operation far longer than Sears' Discover Card. The upcoming analysis will feature all four, with the Sears introduction of the Discover card within the past eight years as particularly indicative of evolving trends among all three credit card operations. The next few sections highlight how these new cultural images were actively formulated through skillful media efforts.

ANALYSIS OF THE 1983 VISA CAMPAIGN

The stage for these repositioned credit card industry services was set by important changes over the last decade. Advertising structured these changes as a total package. The process begins with a theme and subsequently incorporates consumer research, particularly selected marketing goals and objectives, and execution of the actual creative strategy. The following descriptions of specific advertising campaigns illustrate these points.

Visa, formerly known as Bankamericard, repositioned (or created a new public appeal) for its product through formulation of a new name and a strongly enhanced consumer image. Visa, Inc. devised a 1982–1983 advertising campaign around the theme "You can do it. We'd like to help." The campaign included national television, radio, and magazine advertising. The Visa consumer marketing program (Visa, Inc., 1982) projected that "over 95 percent of the Visa target audience will be exposed to the new campaign with each consumer seeing and/or hearing Visa advertising an average of 35 times during the year—a total of nearly 2.5 billion advertising impressions."

Major campaigns such as the Visa effort are created after careful market research. An interview survey consisted of 459 qualified respondents ($25,000 and over, bankcard owner) in 20 metropolitan areas. People were asked about which credit cards would most likely be used by a person with certain characteristics (i.e., often eats out at the best restaurants, shops in specialty more than department stores). Research indicated that Visa was perceived as more appropriate for "luxury/business" purchase decisions, while MasterCard and Visa were perceived as more appropriate for "home and day-for-day" purchases. Visa was generally preferred 0.5:1 over MasterCard and more than 2:1 over American Express for average purchases.

Researchers also examined changing consumer economic and personal attitudes. Visa's analysis observed that baby boomers were entering their peak earning years; the number of working women is at the highest level and still increasing: and an emerging "superclass," consisting of two income couples with no children (often called "DINK" [double income, no kids]) appeared. Husbands and wives have professional managerial jobs in this category.

In the personal area, there was a pronounced trend toward higher education, with 50 percent of college graduates being 25 or older. Greater access to information resulted in more sophistication. The 1982–1983 analysis caught the trend toward more traditional values, as reflected through the maturing of the post–World War II generation. People were marrying at a later age or remarrying in their twenties and thirties; therefore, they were less likely to divorce and likely to strengthen America's social structure.

As a result of this extensive research, the marketing goal was to "improve Visa's position relative to MasterCard and American Express." Marketing objectives for this purpose included strengthening quality image, reinforcing selection of Visa by dual owners (those people possessing MasterCard and Visa-termed *duality* by professionals in the credit card industry), increasing personal and business usage, fostering selection of Visa by nonowners, and stimulating substitution of Visa products for competitive Travel and entertainment cards and checks. The overall key thought to underlie this campaign was that "Visa products can be an important part of the things in life which give Visa prospects the most personal satisfaction." This message was brought out through music, lyrics, and imagery. The marketing program claimed that "the aim of the new campaign is to create a strong, positive emotional bond between the consumer and Visa, and to encourage a preference for Visa products."

Television advertising focused on other aspects of the striving toward fulfillment of our aspirations. Two 60-second commercials and three 30-second commercials, with which two of the 30-second commercials being abbreviated versions of the 60-second versions, were produced. A third 30-second commercial was completely different.

These advertisements presented three situations. The consumer marketing program lists the "stories" as (1) a woman in her forties entering college, overcoming the difficulties, and succeeding; (2) an American couple traveling in Italy and experiencing minor problems while trying to learn the language, then finally becoming comfortable with it; and (3) a family of four buying a very rundown boat, making the necessary repairs, and sailing off.

The theme is visibly presented in three separate "stories" as contained in two 60-second and one 30-second commercial. The first, entitled "Back to School," begins with a quotation attributed to William Arthur Ward: "If you can imagine it, you can achieve it. If you can dream it, you can become it." The actual structure of the advertisement features the wide shot of a college campus. A middle aged woman is shown carrying her books into a classroom. A mature college professor is lecturing in front of the room. The next shot depicts the student in a bookstore line, with the Visa logo prominently displayed on the front counter. Our focus then returns to the college classroom. The professor makes a point, calls on the woman, and then smiles in approval after her reply. At home, the student is writing a term paper while consulting with her husband. The scene finally shifts back into the classroom. The student is taking an examination. In the last sequence, the professor hands back the term papers. The student is surprised, as she apparently receives an "A." She is then surrounded by younger students in jubilant celebration.

The second commercial is a 60-second spot entitled "Europe." The commercial begins with a quotation attributed to Christopher Morley: "There is only one success . . . to be able to spend you life in your own way." The drama begins with two American tourists asking directions. They are then shown seated in an outdoor cafe ordering dinner. The waiter brings them a raw eel on a plate. In the next scene, the couple is riding on a train and asking a question of a nearby couple. A language barrier is evident. The sequence then depicts a financial transaction with Visa traveler's checks understood as a common language. Finally, the couple orders something off a foreign menu. Dinner is served as they had ordered, and both celebrate a successful effort.

The third and last commercial, "Houseboat," was presented as a 30-second ad. A family is shown walking along a dock. They surprise the wife and mother with a rundown boat. The family goes shopping for accessories and then cleans up the craft while experiencing a few minor problems, such as the husband getting doused by a pail of water. Finally, the curtains are hung and the boat, now renamed *WEDIDIT*, is afloat as a recreational vessel.

Each commercial expresses the fulfillment of deeply felt social desires. A woman finds success in a college English course, a married couple encounters language barriers while touring Italy, and a family repairs the rundown boat and sails off into the sunset. These commercials depict the desire for personal freedom and conceptualization of dreams envisioned by consumers.

Magazine ads during 1982 featured inspirational quotations along with the following advertising copy:

Wherever you go, whatever dream you follow, we'd like to help.

Thanks to you, Visa is the most accepted, most widely used name in the world for travel, shopping, and cash.

You can do it. We'd like to help.

Four colorful settings were presented. One setting featured a male fishing at dawn in the middle of a picturesque lake. The quotation, attributed to Christopher Morley, read, "There is only one success . . . to be able to spend your life in your own way." Individuality and freedom of choice are clearly the overriding themes. In the second print ad, two people are setting up camp in the midst of a forest with snow-covered mountain peaks in the background. The quotation, attributed to Thomas Huxley, read, "For every man the world is as fresh as it was the first day, and as full of untold novelties for him who has the eyes to see them." The forest symbolizes a spiritual awakening in the context of a conformist society. The preferred image of achievement and a pioneering spirit is represented in a personal search for identity.

The last two print ads featured other targeted social groups. Whereas the first two ads featured a solitary man and a couple, the other two depict a couple with their infant daughter and a practicing ballerina. The couple and their infant daughter are shown strolling on a tropical beach, with palm trees and the surf in the background. The family is walking along the shoreline. The quotation, attributed to Alfred Lord Tennyson, reads, "So many worlds, so much to do. So little done, such things to do." The last ad shows a ballerina doing a high kick. Her eyes are closed and her arms are extended as she practices in a studio devoid of all furniture but a chair with a towel hanging over its side. The quotation, attributed to Robert Louis Stevenson, reads, "To be what we are, and to become what we are capable of becoming, is the only end of life." These ads are suggesting that we are forever busy in our own worlds seeking accomplishments. The dream of achieving our goals is often proven illusory or deemed unrealistic in a highly competitive society.

MASTERCARD AND MARKETING THE "POSSIBILITIES"

MasterCard was the leading credit card company until the introduction of Visa. The eventual product known as MasterCard was the result of a name change from the original Master Charge. Galonoy (1980) has traced its origins to the Interbank Corporation and its California affiliates back in the 1960s. Mastercharge was not firmly established as a popularly utilized credit card until the William Esty Company, a prominent advertising agency, was awarded the account in 1964. The Interbank Corporation acquired *Master Charge* as a trade name and initiated successive advertising campaigns.

According to a well-placed advertising executive formerly with William Esty, the original emphasis was placed on the utility of Master Charge as a shopping aid. Thus, an early ad featured the slogan "Relax, you've got Master Charge." One of the magazine ads depicted a husband waiting to return from an evening excursion, while another pointed out the dangers of urban crime and the liabilities of carrying cash rather than "plastic money."

Further campaigns over the next 22 years featured a shift from emphasizing the utility of the credit card as a modern social convenience to a focus upon demographic changes and the ways in which the MasterCard could enrich our lives. A particularly successful campaign was launched in the early 1970s, at the height of the women's liberation movement. The slogan was "When you carry Master Charge, you carry Clout." An attractive model was seen holding up a Master Charge card. Laser beams were emanating from the card, indicative of the inherent power of the financial instrument as a weapon enhancing social status. Women were seeking social recognition during this time period. This particular campaign co-opted that ideology in an attempt at harnessing some of the new-found financial power.

Visa (formerly called Bankamericard) entered the marketplace as an active competitor during the late 1970s. The Master Charge organization realized that they needed a more powerful appeal in competing within the same international markets. As a result, Master Charge changed its name to MasterCard. The credit card was not an all-purpose instrument encompassing more than retail services. MasterCard diversified in the early 1980s. The company's advertising campaigns now featured the slogan "'MasterCard and me—we can do it all." The consumer was told that MasterCard could provide a diversified number of services. Subsequent advertising campaigns would feature early versions of the current "Master the Possibilities" emphasis.

A series of commercials featured well-known celebrities utilizing the MasterCard. Christy Brinkley, the fashion supermodel, was shown a new dress (MasterCard, find me a bargain), while other commercials emphasized various commodities. James Coburn, the motion picture actor, was seeking luxurious vacation spots. Pierce Brosnan, formerly the star of *Remington Steele*, was seeking a paradise away from civilization and Shari Belafonte Harper desired a furnished apartment (MasterCard, find me some furniture).

The William Esty advertising agency, in conjunction with the Master-Card organization, followed their success with a series of commercials wherein celebrities interacted with ordinary people. One spot featured an elderly woman sitting next to James Coburn on an airplane. Her statement implied that his search for luxury was merely a reflection of invidious consumption (Veblen, 1983). She claimed that an average person could use the credit card for purchasing wool. A follow up of the Christie Brinkley commercial featured an average woman seeking the same dress worn by the fashion model. The message consisted of the argument that an average women could dress like a supermodel if she used the same credit card.

A subsequent "Master the Possibilities" campaign followed from these previous efforts. Angela Lansbury, Robert Duvall, and the late Jackie Gleason emphasized that they used the card because it served their needs. Lansbury claimed that the card could take her where she wanted, Duvall reinforced the idea that the card was useful in his daily affairs, and Jackie Gleason flaunted his flamboyant lifestyle.

This new campaign was aimed at establishing the potential of consumer credit for expanding our horizons. It should come as no surprise that the appeal of the current commercials is a subdued version of the 1983 Visa commercials. The advertising agency and MasterCard executives are clearly viewing the credit card as a necessary adjunct toward adding further fulfillment within our everyday lives.

The marketing emphasis eventually changed by 1986. The credit card industry showed stagnation when most adults eligible for a MasterCard, Visa, American Express card and other minor cards already had made their choices. MasterCard, Inc. perceived the need for increasing sales through broadened promotional efforts. American Express had just introduced the Optima Card. This instrument would provide installment terms for people already eligible for the American Express Gold card.

First, the advertising account was removed from the William Esty advertising agency. The agency had encountered limited corporate growth and could not provide diversity or the additional attention sought by Master-

Card, Inc.. Barton, Batton, Dane and Osborne (popularly known as BBD&O) was given the multi-million-dollar account.

Second, MasterCard, along with Visa and American Express, targeted college students and housewives as recipients for their credit cards. These groups either could not qualify under previously rigid income or employment experience criteria or did not actively seek out a credit card.

Third, Russell Hogg, corporate executive officer for MasterCard, Inc. since the early 1970s, announced his retirement. The product had a broader consumer and business clientele by late 1987, and Hogg felt that he could pursue other business challenges (Cable Network News, 1988). The new corporate official then worked closely with BBD&O toward fashioning the Gold MasterCard as an alternative for the American Express Gold card. The stakes had shifted into marketing a more prestigious product among the massive consumer sector.

Lintas subsequently assumed and further developed the image created by William Esty and BBD&O. "Master the Possibilities" was transformed into "Master the Moment."[4] The produced television commercials included an emphasis upon buyer protection plans incorporated by the MasterCard Gold card. Advertisements showed a computer accidentally dropped down a flight of stairs and a camcorder dropped into a monkey cage being replaced by merchants honoring the MasterCard Gold card. The most fascinating advertisement in that series featured a woman flying to Australia on the spur of the moment to visit her pregnant sister. The teleplay focused on the woman as she charged her airline tickets and secured a car rental. The outcome was depicted as a touching scene wherein the two sisters warmly embraced one another.

Two other commercials produced within the same advertising campaign demonstrate how a MasterCard can change the lives of ordinary people. In one interesting advertisement, a young man is looking for his first apartment. He decides on a dingy apartment after seeing an attractive woman exit from a nearby apartment. The young man takes a MasterCard and charges furniture, draperies, and other "kitschy" items for an original atmospheric effect. The young woman comes to dinner and exclaims, "This is definitely you."

A second commercial was more appropriate as a nominee for the Soap Opera Awards than a credit card advertisement. A credit card succeeds in solving life's tough problems. A couple are discussing their probable future. The young woman explains that her employer is transferring her to Chicago. The young man continually ponders the loss of his significant other. Finally, he enters a jewelry store and picks out an engagement ring. The young man presents the ring to his girlfriend, and everyone lives happily ever after.

MasterCard changed its advertising again after encountering a cultural economic image problem faced by various credit card companies. The materialist economic trend favoring conspicuous consumption in the 1980s shifted in the direction of practical financial responsibility in the 1990s. According to Elliot (1993), MasterCard's "Master the Moment," wherein conspicuous consumption was the prominent social attitude, was ineffective during times of massive consumer debt and economic retrenchment.

Visa International and Discover were cutting into the MasterCard market share with exclusive events accessible through the Visa card ("Visa—it's everywhere you want to be") and cash rebates (commercials emphasizing a 1 percent cash return based on yearly purchases).

The new marketing campaign emphasized the slogan "MasterCard. It's more than a credit card. It's smart money." According to the Mastercard affiliate marketing material:

This is not just a new theme line, it also happens to be a good one. Because it gives Mastercard a quality people aspire to: feeling smart. They'll feel smart for owning the most useful card, and they'll feel that MasterCard is smarter to use than other credit cards. By using the word "money," the new advertising theme line also makes people feel that MasterCard is more convenient to use than cash. And more responsible. Even . . . smarter.[5]

MasterCard's statements in the press reinforce the marketing theme. According to Peter S. P. Dimsey, president of MasterCard's U.S. region in New York, "We're dealing with a consumer who's looking at credit cards differently. Not as a passport to the good life, as it was in the 80's, but in the ever expanding utility of the card." James Desrosier, vice president of advertising at MasterCard stated, "We call it usefulness, because that's the customer's language. It's useful to take a card to a supermarket or to an automatic teller machine. That's an incredibly relevant message" (Elliott, 1993, p.87).

The commercials are aimed at making the "utility aspects of prosaic plastic interesting" (p.87). The celebrity spokesman is Rob Morrow, the actor who portrayed Dr. Joel Fleischman in the hit CBS series *Northern Exposure*. Rob Morrow serves as the voice-over announcer in the television and radio commercials. The commercials themselves feature Rob Morrow's delivery of "discursive stream of consciousness monologues that manage to sound hip without being arch and clever without being coy. His urbane quirky attitude is reinforced in the television spots with camera shots that are often literally and figuratively off center" (p.87).

The first advertisement is entitled "Supermarket." The advertising copy is presented as follows:

You know those credit card commercials where they tell you to jaunt off to some-place with crystal clear water [beach scene] and really strange fruit and don't bother packing because you can charge everything once you get there? [a couple in beach attire] This isn't one of them, OK? [TV set just turned off] We're taking our Master-Card to the supermarket. How's that for exotic? [Closeup of a MasterCard] Now that you mention it, I guess it is kind of exotic. [Low level shot of a shopping cart] I mean, you've got a MasterCard, and they've got the fruit, right? What's a kumquat? Whatever it is, they're five for a quarter [Shot of a disembodied hand spraying kum-quats] You want crystal clear water? They have aisles full of it. And now no card is more accepted on the planet, including supermarkets. [Shopping cart gliding past a long aisle of bottled water] So you don't have to worry about exact change or losing your receipt or whether you even remembered to record how much your check was for in the first place. [a female cashier mouthing the voiceover narration] It's just an-other smart new way you can use your MasterCard. Only when you get your state-ment you won't have a conniption. [shopping cart traveling through the store] You just have a record of your grocery spending for the month. [closeup of a MasterCard statement itemizing grocery purchases] And a couple of kumquats. [grocery clerk packing the purchases while holding the Kumquats and mouthing the voiceover narration] MasterCard. It's more than a credit card. It's smart money. [Closeup of a MasterCard].

The interesting aspect of this commercial is the postmodern quirkiness. An emphasis on everyday life events (usefulness is the hook that Master-Card employs in demonstrating how credit card utility in everyday life is more practical than the other exotic credit card images) starts with Rob Morrow, whose character image on *Northern Exposure* is that of a New York doctor reluctantly working in a provincial Alaskan town. The camera shots emphasize the ordinary aspects of grocery shopping. Additionally, the se-quences where the cashier and grocery clerks mouth the words bring the viewers more fully into the interaction.[6]

A second advertisement is geared toward "repositioning" (or establish-ing) the utility of the Gold MasterCard. The commercial is entitled "Par-ents":

This is a Gold MasterCard, OK? Sure it's got a credit line of at least five thousand dollars, [close-up of a Gold MasterCard] but it won't settle any unresolved issues from your childhood. [family gathering for a dinner in an upscale restaurant] Well . . . maybe it could. I mean, no gold card is more accepted on the planet [an elderly mother type sitting down at the table] so you can take your parents to dinner practi-cally anywhere [close-up of a father-like male] and say, "Mom, Dad . . . You raised me. I owe you a steak." [a woman toasting her parents] And it might be smart to buy them a grandfather clock to replace the one you demolished when you were eight. [workers wheeling in a grandfather clock wrapped in a large red bow] And if this one gets broken, the MasterPurchase Plan will replace it. [mother type woman is smiling] So I guess a Gold MasterCard could resolve some childhood issues. Wow. [young woman is smiling] Gold MasterCard. It's more than a gold card. It's smart money [close-up of a Gold MasterCard].

The Gold MasterCard commercial is tapping into human feelings. A person can make symbolic restitution or heal family conflict with the aid of the credit card. The postmodern emphasis on the interlink between culture and economic interests clearly is reflected in this teleplay. Spending money and charging the purchases on a credit card incorporate a practical usefulness beyond the pursuit of conspicuous consumption.

Both advertisements create a distinct personality for the MasterCard brand. According to Steve Apesos, marketing director for MasterCard International, the commercials emphasize what is different between Master-Card and the various competitors. In addition, the narrator points out how possessing the credit card may change your life (MasterCard International, 1993).

The MasterCard is useful for more than a few purposes. One radio spot facetiously concentrates on how a MasterCard holder can obtain a better job, while the second focuses on how to meet women. The ad copy almost speaks for itself in pointing out how the credit card can offer career advancement through building a solid credit rating while suggesting ambition and "a sense of direction." Another ad points out that the card may also help a person meet women. The rationale is that you can buy a cute dog and make conversation with women in a supermarket (MasterCard International, 1993).

Both radio spots elaborate on an invented usofulness associated with the MasterCard. Obviously, the television and radio commercials are creating frivolous situations. But the key lies in how the audience perceives the connection between the cultural acceptance of a credit card and the actual economic advantages offered by the MasterCard program. According to Duncan Pollack, executive vice president at Ammirati, "By talking in an earnest, light hearted, down to earth way, the advertising is almost self-effacing, taking the hyperbole of traditional credit card ads and turning it on its head. That enables consumers to put down their barriers, open their ears and begin to listen to MasterCard. And the message is, you're going to be smart for choosing and using Mastercard (Elliott, 1993, p. 87).

AMERICAN EXPRESS: FROM PARANOIA TO AMERICANA

The American Express Company was the pioneer the other companies sought to emulate. The American Express card was established in 1958 as an auxiliary travel aid accompanying the traveler's checks service. Most American Express advertising campaigns from the early 1960s through the early 1980s emphasized the extensive travel services that people could obtain through the card. Travel insurance, emergency cash advances, and security were some of the more prolific foci of these campaigns.

The campaign was basically an offshoot of the popular American Express traveler's checks commercials featuring Karl Malden. The commercials would regularly feature people losing their cash or becoming the victims of criminal assailants. Each commercial would end with these stern words: "What can we do, what can we do?" People would then consult an American Express employee and receive instant cash reimbursement. Karl Malden then reminded the viewers of the following: "Don't let this happen to you. American Express traveler's checks—don't leave home without them."

The credit card commercials carried the same appeal. The card was promoted as a status symbol for the business clientele. Worldwide travel services were emphasized in a focus on dining, hotel bill payments, and security. Like MasterCard, American Express changed with the times. The passage of the Equal Credit Opportunity Act in 1978 produced new American Express initiatives toward seeking out women as potential customers.

Men and women would meet in the context of family outings, business lunches, or casual meetings. The female would pay the check using her newly acquired American Express card. One commercial, emphasizing the singles dating scene, depicted a conversation between two members of the opposite sex. Each would offer small talk while hoping that the other person found them attractive. Thus, we would hear comments like, "You can pick up the tab next time" uttered by the female and a silent "I'm glad there is a next time" flashing through the mind of the male.

The American Express card division sought its own identity in the early 1980s. The campaign theme was "American Express card—part of a lot of interesting lives." This series of commercials featured everyday people going about their lives and utilizing the American Express card. Businessmen, housewives, and average families utilized the card in traveling, shopping, or restaurant dining. A later version of these commercials featured Dick Rutan and Genia Yager, two explorers famous for flying around the world without refueling. The American Express card is prominent in their lives as a vehicle for travel, dining, and meeting hotel expenses.

American Express shifted the focus of its ad campaigns several times over the succeeding years. A 1991 advertising campaign featured the American Express card turning up on airplane tails, appearing on a bridge between a putting green and the fairway, and sitting on a table beside a businessman as he paid for an expensive working dinner. The commercials basically emphasized the utility of American Express cards as an asset while consuming leisure time activities, traveling to another city for business conferences, or wining and dining clients.

The print ads reinforced the major theme. One print ad featured a well-decorated gentleman wearing the American Express card as one of many medallions. The ad read: "You're not about to wear your financial savvy and stability on your sleeve. There are other places." A second print ad depicted an upscale woman contemplating the purchase of an expensive artwork. The ad copy emphasized the familiar impulse buying facilitated by American Express and other credit cards: "Buy what you want to buy. And no bankcard is going to stop you with a limit set long ago. You know what you can afford. You just want to be trusted. You're a responsible person. Most of the time."[7]

Unfortunately, the new advertising campaign was not successful. American Express lost a great deal of market share due to the enhanced competition with AT&T, other affinity cards, and the downscaling of consumer purchases following major debt problems. The AT&T Universal Card and affinity cards offered the same credit privileges as the more established major credit cards. As a result, consumers found themselves rejecting a standard credit card in favor of a card representing their favorite organization or sports team.

The heightened competition for credit card customers and growing consumer debt from credit cards and other forms of consumer credit led to a reformulation of the American Express advertising campaign. American Express turned to other advertising agencies in reformulating its overall approach. The new campaign rejected the postmodern images portrayed in American Express as a force behind everyday business accomplishments. The new focus was on interesting people, harking back to the campaign wherein the Amex card was a part of many interesting lives. Owners of The Body Shop and the Union Square Cafe, two trendy business operations, spoke about concerns for the environment and starving African people (The Body Shop) and cooperation in HarvestFest, a program where surplus food is distributed to homeless people (Union Square Cafe). The card is never mentioned. But American Express is demonstrating that these are two socially conscious businesses that accept the American Express card in everyday transactions.

THE "DAWN" OF DISCOVER

A new credit card was actively marketed with a major advertising campaign initiated in January 1983. Sears, Roebuck and Company began distribution of the Discover Card. Sears found itself in a difficult position. Its retail outlets were already accepting the Sears card and the American Express card. However, Sears was losing retail volume in competition with other leading merchants. The Sears card was underutilized and scarcely returned a profit. The store did not charge an annual fee, and the 21 percent installment charges were not sufficient for the low customer volume. American Express, the other card utilized in Sears stores throughout the country, actually cost the outlet major profits. The merchant fee were approximately 3 percent of each purchase, the highest among MasterCard, Visa, and other accepted cards.

The credit card was administered by the Greenwood Trust Company. Greenwood was a banking entity within the Sears Financial Group. Other components of the group included financial planning (Dean Witter), Caldwell Banker (real estate), and H&R Block (tax specialists). Sears thought that establishing a major financial apparatus would eventually result in major financial gains. As indicated in the chapter on retailing, the major department store chains failed in predicting the establishment of significant competition and worsening economic conditions.

The initial campaign was timed for maximum exposure. Sears placed several major advertisements during the 1983 Super Bowl. Additionally, a newspaper insert was distributed during the same weekend. The television commercials depicted Americans at work and at play throughout the United States. Americans were shown at family gatherings, softball games, individual activities, and other social events. The campaign slogan stressed "the Dawn of Discover." A jingle emphasized that the Discover Card "would put money in a whole new light."

The Discover Card floundered for the first few years. The period between 1983 and 1988 marked a rough maturing process. The Discover Card did not apparently expand Sears' reach in the consumer market. Americans actually applied for the Discover Card. Greenwood Trust Co. reported million of applications after the fist few months. The card offered accompanying features that included automatic investment in a generously paying money market account and a cash back incentive. Consumers using the card qualified for a 1 percent rebates as reimbursement of accumulated purchasing volume after each year. Unfortunately, the 21 percent installment charges were not very popular. The low purchasing volume was marked by lack of Discover Card profitability in another area. The Discover Card did not require an annual fee of $15–$30 for card ownership. Finance charges and annual fees are the traditional profit making devices for the mass distributed credit cards.

Americans were still habitually using American Express, Visa, and MasterCard. Additionally, American Express introduced the Optima card in 1986. The Optima Card was intended for competition in the same market as MasterCard and Visa. The market was already flooded with millions of MasterCards, Visas, American Express Cards, and other department store and minor credit cards. The credit card industry was already hard put for locating additional individuals interested in accepting other available credit cards.

The Discover Card finally made $80 million in 1989 (American Banker, 1990). Earlier reports were already indicating that the Discover Card was having an impact on the already glutted credit card market (American Banker, 1989). The combination of rebates and free membership was responsible for the spectacular success (Blank, 1989). Sears was also seeking out more merchants interested in accepting the Discover Card. According to published sources, Sears established a contest promising a prize for the millionth merchant accepting the card (Shoultz, 1989).

Sears had 31 million credit cards in circulation by 1989 (Kantrow, 1989). But a subsequent survey indicated that the Discover Card was losing ground by the following year (Kantrow, 1990). Sears previously countered this trend by charging an annual fee in Wisconsin and North Carolina (Weiner, 1988). The Discover Card also won the card process contract for Florida Burger Kings (Kantrow, 1989).

Sears made some headway with a new advertising campaign initiated in 1990. They emphasized the millions of dollars in cash rebates paid out to Discover Card users. The campaign may have produced some immediate results. But the financial outlook still seemed rather pessimistic.

New developments emerged in early 1991. Credit card industry rumors indicated that Sears might drop the Discover Card. Sears applied for a Visa card franchise in April (Fitzgerald, 1991; Kantrow, 1991). But MasterCard immediately filed suit claiming the potential creation of a monopolistic situation. Sears resolved the suit by postponing acceptance of Visa cards until the Discover card was sold to another financial corporation.

CONCLUSIONS

O'Connor (1982), Harvey (1989), and Schudson (1985) would endorse the view that shrewd marketing of credit cards enhanced the distribution of commodities. People now had more "bang for the buck" as their economic possibilities were broadened. Advertising is seen as a potential manipulation of American consciousness if we accept this premise. In essence, banks are allied with credit card companies in promoting the sale of merchandise and consumer services. People are seeking economic and social approval while becoming molded by a slick advertising effort.

Advertising has played a significant role in shaping our consumer consciousness. Perhaps Ewen was right in pointing out that we are a product of the culture. Several questions remain in this regard. How are we affected by this increased spending activity as generated by these marketing efforts? What are the economic implications as posed by this drive toward more consumer or cultural capital accumulation? And finally, can the business community anticipate the economic cycles created by perceived consumer commodity needs? These questions are answered in the remaining chapters on retail companies and the cultural economic impact of federal legislation that altered bankruptcy law.

NOTES

1. Leiss, and colleagues, along with Jhally, claim that advertising satisfies particular consumer needs. Advertising imagery, as seen from the more recent postmodern perspective, deconstructs or decodes the meaning behind the images.

2. American Express released a booklet on women and consumer credit shortly after the passage of the Equal Credit Opportunity Act. The purpose of such a booklet and the inclusion of women as credit card holders centered around the need for increasing the numbers of people owning and actively using consumer credit.

3. Further background on agenda setting is contained in a symposium published in the spring 1993, *Journal of Communication*. See McCombs and Shaw (1993, pp. 58–67); Rogers, Dearing, and Bregman (1993, pp. 68–84); Edelstein (1993, pp. 85–99); and Kosicki (1993, pp.100–127).

4. Information relayed by an account executive at BBD&O in a 1992 telephone interview.

5. The affiliate marketing package also mentions that there is pronounced consumer resistance to taking on new debt or accepting a new credit card. The copy in the MasterCard material appeals to these concerns: "Suppose this new ad campaign told people something useful. Something relevant. Something that made them feel smart. Would it really make them do anything? Like apply? Or use MasterCard more often? No question about it." The remainder of this appeal enhances the MasterCard image as a useful product in the lives of consumer spenders.

6. The moving statues and vocal narration at the fountain in the Forum Mall, Caesar's Palace, Las Vegas, Nevada, fulfill the same purpose.

7. Print ads furnished by Ogilvy and Mather (1992) American Express's former advertising agency.

5

Commodity Distribution Networks

The production of consumer goods is only the first step in a more complex process of distribution. Industrial firms can realize financial gains if these goods circulate and produce economic profit. An ongoing supply and demand continuum dictates identification of a market appropriate for a given product. Unlike the Fordist mode of production, potential consumer appeal or demand is assessed before initiating production of the product. Production is accompanied by promotion (e.g., advertising) and distribution.

Public acceptance of retail credit is encouraged through a number of socio-economic developments. Consumer tastes and economic conditions directly affect the retail sector.[1] Overall economic growth is documented through changes in consumer behavior. Changes in product distribution are facilitated by advanced technology and consumer endorsement of alternate purchasing modes. Entrepreneurs exploit varied marketing alternatives created through advances within the retail field. ATMs and computerized credit card systems are two of the technological developments prompting the growing sophistication of retail credit distribution systems. The introduction and simultaneous cultural acceptance of new information technology systems impact on economic production systems and distribution. Retailers rely on a combination of onsite department store sales, catalogs and home shopping services in attaining the desired product distribution. Advanced technology within these distribution modes is rendered more effective through the expansion of flexible specialization and niche marketing for marginal products.

Commodity distribution trends are essential in tracking the effectiveness of niche marketing strategies. Economic reversals among affluent customers in upscale department stores and boutiques and average consumers in department stores and shopping malls explain downturns in the business world. These upper-scale stores have always depended on the affluent to display their conspicuous consumption behavior through purchasing goods and services. For the first time in several decades, department stores appealing to upper-scale consumers are suffering the same fate as department stores catering to middle-class interests.

Retail volume was traditionally concentrated in the on-site department store emporiums. More recently, retailing establishments are divided between the traditional department stores, the so called boutiques, and the discount chains. Boutiques offer specialized selections that are often unavailable in department stores. Boutiques embody niche marketing, wherein the shops are devoted to selling unusual or exclusive clothing, specialized foods, or even condoms.

The average consumer is offered alternative choices in the form of discount retail shopping outlets. The competitive factor is significant because the smaller stores can lower prices while stimulating sales volume. Stores such as *Nobody Beats the Wiz* (a prominent record and electronics chain in the New York Metropolitan Area) significantly reduce department store business.

The current chapter examines trends in department store patronage by consumer groups, the impact of structural changes within the retail market, and the cultural forces responsible for consumer acceptance or rejection of subsequent retailing innovations. Consumers attribute perceived gratification or meaning to particular objects. Everyday portrayal of consumer objects as commodities with experiential references is mediated by advertising and subjective classification.[2] Retailers act as facilitators between the industrial sector (producers) and purchasers of the intended consumer goods (consumers). The development of new retailing technologies and the impact of niche marketing are important factors in explaining various technical changes. Cultural acceptance of new retailing modes enables continued evolutionary change within the retail sector.

An explanation of how technological change in commodity distribution networks affects consumer demand is posited within the role of installment credit, credit cards, and emergent financial transaction systems such as televised home shopping systems. Analysis of these factors accounts for the creation, adaptability, and survival of newly created market segments within a capitalist society.

CULTURAL BASIS OF ECONOMIC TRANSFORMATION

The success of the retail sector is directly linked with cultural expectations formed through the retailer consumer relationship. An understanding of the symbolic nature of the retail transaction begins with a theoretical explanation of the retail process. The capitalist system invents an inherent logic emphasizing the ethics of exchange. Commodities are imbued with a consideration of symbolic capital expressed in equivalent value. Individual value is negotiated by the point of exchange—in this case, the merchant or the larger marketplace. The merchant imposes a particular price (or value) on the particular object. Consumers agree with this assessment and accept the retailer's price. The method of exchange results in a completed exchange between the merchant and the customer. A successful retail exchange places emphasis on "victory" (or the negotiation of these exchange values).[3]

Consideration of two factors, result versus process, creates a linkage between retailing and the institutionalization of consumer credit. The result, as understood by most analyses of this phenomenon, is the realization of a multibillion-dollar industry wherein approximately 50 percent of the transactions are achieved through consumer credit (National Retail Merchants Association, 1986). The sale is symbolically, but not actually, completed at the moment of transaction when consumer credit is utilized as an instrumental tool facilitating the exchange. The business sector, as represented by diverse retail outlets, utilizes the promise of eventual consumer payment in the completion of the immediate transaction.

The consumer is not immediately faced by a predetermined cash limit while in the marketplace. The only limit is imposed by financial institutional credit line limitations.[4] Some credit cards permit more consumer purchasing power than others in the retail sector. Bank credit cards usually carry a specific spending limit. Alternately, American Express has no preset limit. American Express determines customer purchasing limits according to the cardholder's financial ability and previous purchasing patterns.[5]

Constraints on consumer spending were historically removed in other ways. A chain of events emerged that eventually substituted deferred gratification for an orientation favoring instant gratification through consumer purchasing power. Corporations perceived the need for marketing durable goods and other immediately unaffordable produced commodities. A tie-in between the manufactured product and other essential services with weekly wages and a local structure providing everyday needs fulfilled the corporate marketing goals.

Historical examples include Henry Ford's then innovative plan for making automobiles immediately affordable for the average worker and an equally noteworthy system in "company towns." Company towns (as situated in the Chicago-based George Pullman industrial operation) provided an instantly available workforce. The workers were totally dependent on Pullman's commercial establishment for their everyday survival. The cost of medical care, living quarters, and food provisions were automatically deducted from the small weekly salary earned by the workers.[6] Such company towns continued until the development of larger cities and the affordability of the automobile (or development of public transportation systems). Railroad car production ceased with the Pullman plant's closing in the 1940s.

The concept known as "Fordism" (or mass production of a particular product on an assembly line) originated with Henry Ford's mass production factory system. Henry Ford, a capitalist entrepreneur associated with the development of the automobile industry, also embodied the exploitation exacted by George Pullman. Henry Ford's plan was much more subtle. Ford was credited with industrial reforms, which included shortened working hours and higher employee salaries. His rationale was based on the idea that automobile assembly-line workers were a natural market for the automobiles produced through their own labor. These workers could purchase the product with the wages generated from these industrial efforts, utilize an installment plan in providing immediate affordability and product availability, and rationalize the purchase with an understanding that a shorter work-week allowed sufficient leisure time toward maximizing the automobile's utility.

Interesting parallels exist in the 1980s. The ultimate success of the retail sector was dependent on increased elaboration of a complex technostructure, wherein individuals contribute expertise to the implementation and management of consumer credit systems (Galbraith, 1975). Daniel Bell's (1976a) discussion of the postindustrial society predicted this trend in an analysis of the growing service industry. Financial records and collection procedures became a specialized bureaucratic system ensuring the profitability of the consumer credit apparatus.

Retail outlets are the backbone of the consumer credit industry. Retailers are distributors and customers. The retail industry is a major supplier of consumer goods and major customer of the credit card companies. The various department stores, starting with Sears, Roebuck and Co. and including smaller neighborhood establishments, can market their own credit cards and installment accounts and/or accept nationally distributed credit cards as distributed through financial institutions. The mechanics of these arrangements are more fully discussed in a later portion of this chapter.

Credit cards provide convenience and satisfy ongoing purchase demands. First, convenience is provided through obtaining consumer items and rendering payment at a more convenient time. The retailer receives payment from the credit card users within a week. The consumer can pay in full or send in small partial payments. Second, consumer purchase demands are satisfied through credit utilization at any particular time. Consumers need not wait until savings are accumulated before obtaining the desired merchandise. The consumer credit industry encouraged growth of the retail sector. The use of revolving and installment credit fulfills a desire for durable and other heretofore unaffordable goods. Actual development of the retail industry and its impact on American society are chronicled in the next section.

GROWTH OF THE RETAIL SYSTEM

The development of retailing reflects the evolution of consumer credit in American society. Robert Johnson, director of the Credit Research Center, Purdue University, has reported on the origins and trends associated with retail credit. According to Johnson (1980), the function of retail credit is oriented toward the maximization of business profits. Added service revenues permitted the retailer to charge less for the merchandise through generation of additional sales volume.[7] Installment credit, as a precursor to credit cards, directed consumers toward the acceptance of contemporary credit instruments.[8]

Johnson traces the history of retail credit back to colonial times with the utilization of open book accounts.[9] Consumers made an informal promise that they would settle the account at a future time. Farmers, dependent on industrial firms for machinery and domestic products, paid their entire accounts when the crops came in. Retailers in industrial and commercial areas expected partial payment each month. Creditors were not charged for this service. The cost of credit was incorporated as part of the merchandise selling price.

Open book accounts were forerunners for the current credit systems. Customers and merchants entered into an understood agreement. The small general stores were instrumental in providing basic food and merchandise supplies. Trust was implied within the business relationship. Credit transactions were noted in a book. Customers could pick up the merchandise and pay the store owner at a later date.

Open book credit was generally restricted to farmers, planters, and relatively affluent city dwellers. The average citizen was not given these privileges until after the Civil War. Open book accounts had limited utility for these consumers. The small purchases were convenient, but credit needs were greater with the financing of durable goods. A single payment would not handle the cost of such costly consumer items as sewing machines and furniture. This factor stimulated the issuance of installment credit.

Johnson supplied a comprehensive background accounting for the beginning of consumer credit. He noted that retail installment credit was first introduced in 1807 by a furniture firm known as Cowperthwaite and Sons.[10] Smock (1962, p.89) offers a rationalization for the establishment of installment selling. Smock claims that "big ticket items" were expensive, and the merchant was reluctant to tie up capital. The consumer found that expensive furniture and major purchases were more affordable through the invention of installment credit.

A formal contract between the parties constituted a legally binding agreement. Installment selling became popularly accepted. The Singer Sewing Machine Company used the installment plan in 1850,[11] and manufacturers of pianos, encyclopedias, and stoves utilized the retail installment arrangements in the 1870 and 1900s.[12] The automobile was also sold in this manner, affording the consumer a chance to purchase these mass-marketed products.

Bass (1977, p.106) observed that a shift from the general store into the modern department store supported the shift from open-book accounts into installment selling. Consumers receiving offers for these convenient 30 day charge accounts possessed higher incomes, worked in white collar occupations, and had substantial bank accounts.[13] Bass[14] further observed that:

Until installment selling had become wide-spread in other areas of consumer selling, most retail stores considered credit to be a costly necessary service and though they reluctantly appreciated the need for open accounts they shied away from installment credit long after other vendors had accepted it. Reputable retailers, especially department stores, did not look favorably upon installment selling and for much of the consuming public, enjoying the use of goods while paying for it was not considered respectable. (p.106)

Bass reports that expansion in retail charge account credit began in the mid-1920s as retail store owners legitimated credit arrangements as an important instrument in competition between retail outlets and between consumer products (p.107). Products sold on installment plans competed with products offered on a cash basis. Bass cites Federal Reserve figures in arguing that open charge accounts have grown steadily since the 1920s. According to Federal Reserve findings, retail credit grew from $1.5 million in 1929 to $10 million in 1974. However, charge account credit has declined in proportion to revolving account plans and bankcards.

Convergence of the economic and cultural aspects of everyday living was expressed in materialistic terms. A shift in cultural values encouraged a realignment of the industrial sector. Bass points out that American consumer attitudes toward consumer credit began to shift (p. 107).[15] Installment buying was made available to consumers with lower incomes. In effect, Bass documents the transformation in retail credit: installment buying transformed retail credit from an arrangement of prestige and convenience for the well-to-do to a means of expediting sales of factory-made goods to consumers on a mass scale" (p. 108). Bass's discussion implies that consumer credit underwent a transformation from an elitist consumer credit system into the "democratization of consumer credit."[16] The actual process began with simple cultural expectations not conducive to the sale of expensive durable goods. But World War I and the rise of the middle class marked an important time in the development of the consumer credit industry.[17]

Bass continues her discussion of the reasons accounting for wider acceptance of consumer credit. She quotes Dauten (1956, p. 11) as claiming that the basic cause of increased investment in consumer durables (and the subsequent rise in consumer credit volume) was attributable to "the fundamental social economic changes associated with industrialization and urbanization" (Bass, 1977, p. 108).[18]

Retailers built up a prejudice against installment selling.[19] An understanding of how retailer attitudes were transformed involves the automobile. The potential of installment selling as a merchandising tool was not realized until the development of the mass-produced automobile. The automobile as an everyday consumer purchase and durable product "brought respectability to installment financing. Consumer purchase of automobiles on installment financing led to credit expansion into other areas of retail credit selling" (p. 110). Major sales finance companies were created with the rise in mass automobile sales demand.

Bass observed that the legitimate recognition of consumer credit coincided with the culmination of the Great Depression and a lifting of wartime credit restrictions.[20] Consumers and retailers gradually recognized that cultural attitudes were changing and the acquisition of durable goods was more accepted. Installment sales were initially applied to certain types of hard goods and required sizable downpayments. But reliance was increasingly placed more on buyers' character and evidence of willingness to pay than on security of the retail transaction.

ADVENT OF THE DEPARTMENT STORE

The rise of urbanization meant a new constituency requiring furnishings and other everyday items. Department stores were tailor-made for accommodating important demographic shifts within American society. The rise of families and steady movement from the urban areas to affluent suburban areas accounted for the utility of these large commercial establishments. Retailing establishments were created for the purpose of showcasing of consumer goods. Consumers found an advantage in having various commodities under one department store roof rather than dispersed among different retail establishments.

The combination of a larger economic structure responsible for transforming and tapping into cultural values and defining social status acted as a significant force.[21] Proponents of the economic system emphasize the rationality of the marketplace as incorporating the production, distribution, and sale of consumer goods or services. A main analytical thread incorporates an understanding of retail industry development and the impact of cultural or technological change. Any systematic study of retail marketing includes a detailed analysis of the retail industry and its structural development. The focus of this analysis features an emphasis on department and chain stores in urban and rural settings, a significant population shift into suburban settings and creation of the "mall culture," and a final metamorphosis into an automated system featuring electronic fund transfers and ATMs.[22]

An understanding of consumer credit and the retail marketing apparatus requires an explanation in terms of cultural and industrial positioning within the technostructure (Bell, 1976a; Bluestone and Harrison, 1982). Bell explained how cultural values were rearranged for the convenience of economic development. He does not see this as a conspiracy; rather, he sees this as a logical extension of consumer desires toward improving their lives through acquiring material objects. Bluestone and Harrison describe how flexible specialization enabled the expansion of industrial growth. Varying consumer needs were addressed through the capability for producing mass products.[23]

Indirect side effects inevitably affected consumers engaged in purchasing and creating these goods. Cultural change in turn affected the composition of a growing working-class sector. New retail opportunities were created through redefined technological abilities and a redeployment of retailing specialists. Bluestone and Harrison pointed out that technological change created a need for replacing workers with others having more appropriate training. In many cases, jobs were declared obsolete and workers were faced with necessary retraining.

Retail marketing is a vital link in the development of department stores, boutiques, and discount stores. Retail marketing, in combination with the development of consumer credit plans, solidified the place of department stores in American society. An analysis of the historical progression of these events explains the impact of these changes on consumer activity. Early consumer credit plans encouraged the cultural transformation from delayed gratification to immediate gratification. The history of modern retail credit plans began shortly before World War II. In 1938, Wanamaker's applied the first department store revolving credit arrangement. A four-month payment period was allowed, and no charge was made for credit. Revolving credit was restricted during World War II by Regulation W. The economic boom after the war was accompanied by installment credit plans with assessed finance charges.[24] Two plans were previously available. Retailers offered a 30 day charge account and the installment account. The 30 day charge account was a free service, provided that the consumer paid within that time period. The installment account typically included a 6 percent finance charge.

The next step in the process was characterized by the rapid growth of the department store. Urbanization of the American population prompted a consumer dependence on mass-marketed goods. Development of urbanization and the formation of competing retail outlets are two factors reflected in an analysis of leading department stores. The stores are predominantly located in major urban areas. A large population depended on the major retailing firms for desired consumer items. Each store carved its own niche in the surrounding community. As a result, these stores developed into long-standing businesses, with succeeding generations forming a steady clientele.

The early department stores supplied sought-after consumer goods and stimulated the production of these commodities in the United States. Additionally, these department stores fulfilled the need in centralizing the availability of goods and services under one roof. These early department stores were grand palaces catering to the wealthy or upwardly mobile. Bloomingdale's, Saks Fifth Avenue, B. Altman, and Macy's were among the more noted retailing outlets renowned throughout the United States.[25]

The leading department stores attained impressive economic growth. Hendrickson (1974, p. 458) categorizes department stores according to several criteria. First, he lists ten department stores according to overall volume in 1977. These firms were ranked as follows: (1) Macy's (New York); (2) Hudson's (Detroit)—since out of business; (3) Abraham and Straus (Brooklyn); (4) Broadway (Los Angeles); (5) Marshall Field (Chicago); (6) Korvettes (New York)-since out of business; (7) Bamberger's (New Jersey)—a subsidiary of Gimbel's and now out of business; (8) Alexander's (New York)—also out of business; (9) May Company (California); and (10) Bloomingdale's (New York).

Hendrickson lists 22 retail chains accounting for sales ranging from $22 billion to $1 billion. These firms were ranked as follows: (1) Sears Roebuck $22.024 billion; (2) K Mart $10.064 billion; (3) JC Penney $9.369 billion; (4) FW Woolworth $5.543 billion; (5) Montgomery Ward $5 billion; (6) Federated Department Stores $4.923 billion; (7) Winn-Dixie Stores $3.997 billion; (8) Lucky Stores $3.974 billion; (9) American Stores $3.465 billion; (10) May Department stores $2.370 billion; (11) Dayton-Hudson Stores $2.191 billion;

(12) Rapid-American $2.046 billion; (13) Allied Stores $1.927 billion; (14) RH Macy $1.661 billion; (15) Gamble-Skogmo $1.634 billion; (16) Carter Hawley Hale $1.505 billion; (17) Associated Dry Goods $1.468 billion; (18) McCrory Corporation $1.350 billion; (19) Zayre Corporation $1.261 billion; (20) Geneseo $1.015 billion; (21) Gimbel's $1 billion; and (22) Vornado $1 billion (p. 458).[26]

Hendrickson indicated the 13 most profitable department store chains.[27] The retailing outfits and their profit margins in 1978 are listed as follows: (1) Sears Roebuck $836 million; (2) K Mart $302.9 million; (3) JC Penney $295 million; (4) Federated Department Stores $196.6 million; (5) FW Woolworth $91.9 million; (6) May Department Stores $84 million; (7) Dayton-Hudson $84 million; (8) Allied Stores $74.2 million; (9) Winn-Dixie $70 million; (10) Lucky Stores $61.3 million; (11) Macy's-$52.8 million; (12) Carter Hawley Hale $50.1 million; and (13) Associated Dry Goods-$42.1 million (p.459).

The 11 richest department store chains were also listed in the Hendrickson study: (1) Sears, Roebuck $23.086 billion; (2) Mobile Oil (Montreal) $20.579 billion; (3) JC Penney-$4.106 billion; (4) K Mart $3.428 billion; (5) Federated Department Stores $2.520 billion; (6) FW Woolworth $1.214 billion; (7) May Department Stores $1.651 billion; (8) Arlen Realty Stores (Korvettes) $1.563 billion; (9) Rapid American $1.485 billion; (10) Allied Stores $1.295 billion; and (11) Dayton-Hudson-$1.219 billion (p.459).[28]

The credit card figured prominently in the enhancement of department store profitability. More than 50 percent of overall sales were attributed to consumer utilization of either a store charge card or a major credit card. Credit cards also facilitated the increase in unanticipated (or impulse) shopper purchases.

These statistics on department store profitability indicate the prosperous nature of the retail industry. Profitability margins may change depending on outside leveraged investments[29] or the overall economic situation. The 1993 Macy's acquisition is one such example. The company acquired Bullock's and other expensive retail properties. But this trend is one factor useful for understanding the expansion of overall retail chains. The retail industry has always had a consistent core of customers. Problems arose with greed from overexpansion and competition from within the industry itself. The story of shopping malls and teleshopping completes the overall picture.

CREATION OF THE "MALL CULTURE"

The mall culture was an artifact of social change. Urban and suburban areas experienced a concentrated population shift. Central areas for shopping, recreation, and social functions were welcomed by area residents. The establishment of shopping malls in suburban areas was especially important. Major population segments relocated from urban to suburban areas. Residents in suburbia needed retail stores for food, clothing, and other essential services. Suburban dwellers possessed middle-or upper-income resources. Financial worth was supplemented by adequate consumer or retail credit lines. The combination of a sizable consumer cohort and their spending potential encouraged the growth of shopping malls. Jacobs (1984) documented the growth of shopping malls. There were 16,400 shopping centers in 1975 and 22,750 in 1981.[30]

Jacobs (p. 1) cites Feagin (1982) in noting that shopping centers account for about half of all annual retail sales in the United States involving general merchandise and clothing. The growth of the shopping center industry is interesting because the first large regional shopping centers were not built until the 1950s.

The early shopping centers were built around a core of major department stores. Nine out of ten shopping malls in the early 1980s were less than ten years old. The post-World War II era was important in encouraging the relocation of major retail businesses. America witnessed a level of consumption unknown in prior generations and not seen since. Retail credit and consumer credit cards were more available than at any other time period. Jacobs explains that the modern shopping mall was an expansion of urban arcades established in the nineteenth century (pp. 1–2). According to Gruen (1973), early shopping malls were observed in Athens, Roman forums and oriental bazaars. More contemporary examples in the pre–World War II period included the development of suburban shopping facilities in the 1930s and 1940s. Two were the Country Club Plaza in Kansas City, Missouri, and Westwood Village in Los Angeles. These early shopping malls concentrated on offering office space rather than large department stores.

As previously noted, the flight from urban areas to suburbia was encouraged by the development of the automobile. Enhanced transportation capabilities enabled the construction of suburban communities. New highways and large parking lots accommodated the heavy traffic patterns. Merchants and department store owners relocated from downtown areas into the new population centers. Customers offered relatively affluent income levels and sufficient consumer credit capability.

According to Hendrickson (1974), the world's biggest shopping centers were: Lakewood Center, Lakewood, California; Woodfield Mall, Schaumburg, Illinois; Randall Park, Cleveland, Ohio; Roosevelt Field, Garden City, New York; Cinderella City, Engelwood, California; Metrocenter, Phoenix, Arizona; and Yorktown Shopping Center, Lombard, Illinois. The seven states with the most shopping centers are California, 2,044; Texas, 1,470; Florida, 988; New York, 868; Ohio, 737; Pennsylvania, 730; and Illinois, 628

(p.461). The states listed above encompassed large suburban areas and substantial population size.

The shopping mall sustained its appeal through offering a broadened array of services. According to Rybczynski (1993), the new shopping malls
constitute ersatz urban centers equipped with post offices, hotels, counseling centers, and theme parks in a weather-protected, safe, and clean place.[31]
Rybcznski's account conjures up images of Zukin's (1991) account of urban
settings as landscapes of power. He claims that there were more than 8,000
new shopping centers opened in the United States from 1960 to 1970, twice
as many as in the previous decade. From 1970 to 1990, about 25,000 new
shopping centers were built in the United States.

Aside from the standard description of prototypical shopping malls es-
tablished in the early part of this century in Chicago, Kansas City, Dallas,
and San Diego, Rybczynski (1993) refers to the more recent malls as larger
and more autonomous. Several more recently opened malls are the Del
Amo Fashion Center in Torrance, California (3 million square feet), the
West Edmonton Mall in Alberta, Canada (5.2 million square feet), and the
Mall of America in Bloomington, Minnesota (4.2 million square feet). The
Mall of America attracts approximately 100,000 people a day. According to
the owners, the Mall of America will attract more visitors than Walt Disney
World or the Grand Canyon. It includes 4 major department stores, ap-
proximately 360 specialty stores, and more than 40 restaurants and food
outlets. The stores are grouped around a seven-acre glass roofed courtyard
containing an amusement park with 23 rides, two theaters, and dozens of
smaller attractions. The courtyard is described as a theme park (Camp
Snoopy, with "counselors" wearing distinctive uniforms). In addition, the
complex includes two hotels. In comparison, the older West Edmonton
Mall "merely" included a skating rink, amusement park, an aviary, a dolphin pool, an artificial lagoon with a submarine ride, a floating replica of
the Santa Maria, and the world's largest indoor water park, complete with
an artificial beach and rolling surf (p. 102).

Credit cards are an important feature of the recent "mega" shopping
malls. A customer visiting the Mall of America probably requires a credit
card if contemplating a multi day stay in one of the nearby hotels. Additionally, credit cards facilitate the numerous consumer purchases during a
protracted shopping trip, as consumers do not carry large amounts of cash.

CONTEMPORARY DEVELOPMENT OF THE RETAIL
INDUSTRY

Shopping malls thrived while consumer credit expenditures increased
and consumer demand remained constant. New business initiatives damp-
ened the growth of urban shopping mall locations. Prosperous operating

results continued until the coming of boutiques and discount outlets offering specialized services or competitive discount prices. Boutiques siphoned away the upper-class consumer trade, while discount outlets tapped into the lower- and middle-class customer base. The major department stores encountered significant competition from boutiques and other discount chains. Boutiques offered specialized clothing, appliances, or products for a select population.

Discount stores also offered the same merchandise as department stores. Discount chain operation success was assured with competitive pricing, locations in more urban and suburban areas, and greater sales volume. This section offers an analysis of how department stores inspired niche marketing (also known as flexible specialization or accumulation) through whetting consumer appetites for various consumer products.[32] Further, the opening of new retailing markets inspired industrial expansion and produced a significant impact on the original department stores and their competitors.[33]

Traditional department stores served general consumer needs. Furniture, household appliances and supplies, clothing, electronics and assorted consumer products were all available under one roof.[34] Boutiques specialize in specific items not offered by department stores. For example, small retailing operations cater to narrow consumer interests. One such store offers products solely intended for cats and cat owners. The boutique sells special cat food, cat care products, and even videos for cats. Cat owners can purchase potholders, refrigerator magnets, statues and other home decorations, and various household accessories decorated with feline images. The shop receives much public attention in newspapers and electronic media reports.[35]

On the other hand, discount stores are an antithesis of the selective boutique merchandising strategy. Discount stores carry a wide variety of consumer goods in particular merchandising lines. For example, discount stores in the electronic business offer savings on videocassette recorders, camcorders, computers, tape recorders, cameras, and other related merchandise.[36]

The catalog business was a traditionally strong adjacent marketing tool for the retail industry. There are a number of retail companies dependent on the catalogue mail order business. A cursory check of some catalogs received or collected by this author includes the following retail businesses: Bloomingdale's (furniture, clothing, and jewelry), 47th Street Photo, Frank Eastern Co. (office furniture), Smythe & Co. (men's and women's clothing), Undergear ("a handbook of activewear and underwear from around the world"), International Male (male clothes and accessories), Frederick's of Hollywood (predominantly women's underwear, outerwear, and accessories), and *Playboy* (clothing, video materials, and numerous items linked with *Playboy* magazine's sensual image).

Notice that this list does not even include the leading retail market catalogs produced by Sears, Roebuck and Co., JC Penney, and Montgomery Ward. The catalog business was predicated on a cultural image presented within and fulfilled by the mail-order operation as a "wish list."[37] A solicitation received from JC Penney points out the advantages of mail-order shopping. The company contends that the JC Penney catalog saves the consumer time and money, makes shopping easier, offers convenient delivery, and provides diverse selection.

The catalogs were popular during a time when the predominantly rural population needed more than the general stores could supply. Sears, Penney, and Montgomery Ward catalog operations formed the equivalent of modern department stores, boutiques, discount chains, suburban shopping malls, and televised home shopping services. The previously cited sales volume statistics lend support to the historical importance of mail-order businesses.

Sears invoked its own form of post-Fordist industrial development through diversified product lines and flexible specialization. The post-Fordist period did not sufficiently evolve until the time period following World War II. It is important to remember that the early 1900s (approximately 1920 to 1930) were a time when the assembly line produced standardized products.

Consumer demand was quite heavy from the late 1800s through the early 1900s. Since the level of consumer demand was uncertain, the Sears assembly line produced a limited supply of goods.[38] The wave of consumer orders overwhelmed the company. Sears factory operations were upgraded with the inclusion of an expanded goods inventory. Some reasons for these changes and the cultural and economic impact of retail marketing are accounted for in the next section. More recently, Montgomery Ward shut down their catalog operation. The combination of ubiquitous shopping malls, home shopping on cable television, and boutiques siphoned off the traditionally heavy consumer-buying volume.

MARKETING CONSUMER CREDIT THROUGH MASS MEDIA

We have previously discussed how the consumer credit industry is instrumental in prompting significant cultural changes within everyday social interaction. Cultural changes in our attire, automobile choices, or travel plans are based on marketed choices. Active marketing promotion is a prerequisite to consumers fitting the product into their everyday lifestyles. Advertising serves an important role in stimulating consumer desire for particular products. Consumer goods are the mainstay of an economic system dependent on elaborate marketing strategies directed toward predetermining cultural acceptance. Successful marketing is the key to achieving maximum profits. Retail markets require efficient distribution networks for the dissemination of the available goods and services. Promotion through television or newspaper advertising is not enough. Bringing products into the marketplace is extremely crucial in achieving this success. The product must reach the marketplace and become accessible through convenient outlets. Department stores and shop-by-mail or phone services make these items directly accessible to the public.[39]

The allure of an expanded consumer marketplace masked the "price" (e.g., technical obsolescence) that societal members faced for this diversity. Ewen (1988) referred to style and the coercion of cultural forces.[40] Mass media emerged as a vital factor in distributing ideological messages along with the diversified consumer products. People are no longer limited to excursions into shopping malls or department stores. Mass marketing is now more sophisticated and widespread than at any point in the twentieth century. The television medium expanded with its utilization of innovative techniques incorporating promotion of merchandise through home shopping programming and brief advertising messages (e.g., "800" numbers).

Televised shopping resources developed in correspondence with the cable industry. Some of the first retail marketing efforts were advanced with "800" telemarketing numbers. Ted Turner, in the early stages of promoting WTBS as a superstation,[41] accepted advertising from telemarketing firms. Kitchen appliances, recordings, and other consumer goods were advertised by firms requesting credit card orders. Telephone operators recorded the orders for processing by the retail company.

The combination of credit cards, televised advertising, and telephone ordering formed an important connection. Consumers now possessed the opportunity for ordering merchandise in the privacy of their own homes. Although home shopping was not new,[42] the combination of media and marketing transcended catalog orders and moved into the visual realm. It was a matter of time before a totally visual home shopping service would tap into the lucrative consumer credit market.

DEVELOPMENT OF THE HOME SHOPPING NETWORK

Mail order through catalogs and television offers remained a viable industry. According to Hawk (1988), 1986 sales were about $135 billion, with consumer mail order at $62 billion, business mail order at $38 billion, and charitable mail order at $35 billion. The mail-order industry experienced some losses in the early part of the 1993 recession. Montgomery Ward's closure caused a $1 billion gap. Growth was pronounced for sportswear, videocassettes, mutual funds, and cable home shopping. The Home Shopping Network (HSN) was one of the major companies with high growth productivity.

The Home Shopping Network was established on July 1, 1985, by Roy Speer and Bud Paxson. The first (HSN) was launched on a nationwide programming, live, 24-hour basis. The Home Shopping Network was an extension of the Home Shopping Club (HSC), which began broadcasting on cable systems in the Tampa Bay area of Florida in July 1982. The HSN launched a second, live, 24-hour network on March 1, 1986. HSN acquired Stuart McGuire Company, a telemarketing outlet, on July 23, 1986. Stuart McGuire handled the overflow calls for the two HSN channels and orders for merchandise from HSN's ten mail-order catalogs. HSN announced the formation of a national broadcast network and began acquiring TV stations in the top TV markets in the US in August 1986. On December 17, 1986, HSN announced the formation of the short-lived Home Shopping Game show syndicated by MCA TV Enterprises for airing in June 1987. On January 7, 1987, HSN announced construction of new studios and corporate facilities on 26 acres of land in St. Petersburg, Florida. These studios were to hold 2,000 telemarketing operators engaged in receiving phone orders.

Hawk (1988) pointed out the reasons for HSN growth and the derivation of the organization's basic telemarketing appeal:[43]

As a sales vehicle, TV has a lot going for it—locale, familiarity, and a reputation for information and entertainment. The big drawback, until recently, has been the limited opportunity for direct customer response. But since HSN went national with its home shopping service in 1985, the TV studio has become an inbound telemarketing machine, creating the impulse to buy and take telephone orders on the spot. (p. 26)

Home Shopping Network had numerous cable competitors for the same telemarketing services. The primary competitors were Cable Value Network (CVN) and Quality Value Cable (QVC). The latter was owned by Sears, Roebuck and Co. and offered Sears merchandise. QVC later added an affinity credit card to offer its customers.

HSN and its competitors capitalized on impulsive consumer spending and a potentially unlimited audience. A 1987 consumer survey sponsored by HSN revealed who watches telemarketing shows. Females are the targeted audience. Teleshopping shows are watched in 52 percent of total U.S. homes, 76 percent of the sampled households watched HSN, and 52 percent of the sampled households watched teleshopping on cable television. The average age of female teleshoppers in total U.S. homes was 39.4 years, HSC shoppers averaged 45.3 years, and general cable TV teleshoppers averaged 40.1 years.

Incomes for teleshoppers in total U.S. homes was $24,897, $39,140 in homes where HSC was viewed, and $35,500 in homes where viewers watched any teleshopping shows. Many of these female teleshoppers were high school graduates. Seventy-three percent of teleshoppers in total U.S. homes were college graduates, 88 percent of the HSN teleshoppers were high school graduates, and 79 percent were general cable TV teleshoppers. The audience was relatively educated. Thirty-four percent of female teleshoppers in total U.S. homes attended college versus 42 percent of the HSC teleshoppers and 40 percent of the general cable teleshoppers. Interestingly, 58 percent of the female teleshoppers in total U.S. homes were employed, 65 percent of the HSC teleshoppers were employed, and 60 percent of the general cable television shoppers were employed (Hawk, 1988, p.26).

Hawk also supplies several other interesting facts. The total number of HSN shoppers includes more than 3 million active home shopping club households. The profile of HSN shoppers includes the following details: 84 percent own a home, 75 percent are suburbanites, and the rest are fairly split between cities and rural areas. The typical customer watches HSN 1.7 hours per day, out of a total TV viewing time of 6.5 hours on weekdays and 8.4 hours on weekends.

The sales figures were also very impressive. Hawk points out that the HSN demonstrates the motivation power of TV shopping shows. HSN sales reached $64 million in the first eight months after nationwide cablecasting in July 1985. Sales reached $1 billion in 1988. Hawk says that the HSN shows about 10 products per hour, netting $1,200 per minute in sales on weekdays and $2,000 per minute on weekends. Order stations are staffed by 2,000 human operators per shift. Tootie, a computerized voice-response system, takes more than 100,000 calls per day.

HSN, Inc. is a very profitable business operation. HSN's teleshopping operation increased 129 percent to $26.2 million in 1987, while earnings per share went from $0.15 cents to $0.29. HSN also expanded from one cable channel to two channels, followed by a larger studio and telesales capacity in several locations. Additionally, Hawk and others state that HSN is engaged in acquiring local UHF stations in urban areas throughout the United States and affiliates in other cities. Hawk reports that HSN gives 5 percent of its revenues to the stations that carry the network— a total of more than $21 million as of 1987. Additionally, HSN maintains several catalogs, and private-label merchandise under 70 labels and is moving into necessities, adding insurance, discount prescription drugs, cosmetics, travel, and financial services.

Other statistics are equally impressive. Agnew (1987) estimated that television home shopping would reach $7.2 billion by 1991. By the end of 1987, 50 million Americans, or 50 percent of all homes with sets, were able to shop by television. Of the 6 percent of cable subscribers who buy from home shopping programs, 64 percent purchase monthly; 66 percent watch more than one hour a week, 71 percent spend more than $20 per purchase, and 48 percent have bought from catalogs in the past six months. HSN had $106 million in sales and 350,000 regular customers in its first nine months. The company also bought ten broadcast stations.[44]

Credit cards are a vital economic component of the Home Shopping Network. Viewers preregister their credit card numbers in the HSN computer and draw on their line of credit when purchasing a particular item. The HSN system benefits from consumer credit card utilization because cash resources are readily transferred into the corporate account. Additionally, consumers can purchase items on an impulsive basis in the same way that shoppers do in a department store.

CONCLUSIONS

Economic resources (e.g., credit cards) permit the consumption of cultural artifacts in the form of symbolic capital (or commodities). Acquisition of cultural objects implies the achievement of particular social statuses.[45]

Home shopping seemingly exploits the impulsive nature of consumer behavior. Shoppers are offered "bargains" and given a high-pressure sales pitch. The viewers must purchase the items within a set time or lose the purchasing privilege. An argument can be posited that consumers are chasing material success through real or symbolic capital. But where does this all lead? The next chapter deals with the cultural interpretation of such behavior as measured through indebtedness and legislative relief.

NOTES

1. The yearly Christmas season accounts for at least 40 percent of the overall yearly retail gain. The everyday progress of consumer spending trends is charted by the nightly network news programs and newspapers. Consumer activity was particularly noteworthy in 1991. President George Bush attempted to prime consumer activity by example: President Bush and his wife Barbara purchased socks and other small items while shopping in a busy suburban mall.

2. The impact of advertising and industrial assertion of economic goals was discussed in more detail in earlier chapters.

3. Bellah, et al. (1985) might assert that individual choice is forfeited while substituting implicit consumer acceptance of the retailer's economic assessment.

4. "Maxing out" is a phrase coined by the business community to describe consumers who have reached their pre-existing credit lines through overzealous purchasing activity.

5. The previous discussion of American Express card advertising demonstrated how this card was presented as a consumer convenience over regular credit cards.

6. A tour of the former Pullman Town was conducted by Philip Nyden, a well known sociologist specializing in Industrial Sociology, during the 1984 annual meeting of the Association for Humanist Sociology.

7. The economic principle of initiating consumer credit and passing the costs (of finance charges) on to the buyers still remains intact. Any extra added costs borne by the merchants (e.g., discount charges from 3 to 6 percent payable to the credit card companies for the licensing privilege) are compensated for by the convenience afforded consumers and attendant sales volume.

8. These points are further detailed by Robert Smock (1962). Smock detailed the impact of rapid industrialization and documented the impact of modern debt on twentieth-century families.

9. Smock (1962) differentiated between open book credit and installment selling. Smock wrote the following regarding these two economic developments:

Installment selling usually differed from open-book credit in that (a) a contract was signed for a specific major purchase, (b) the contract established a conditional sale with payments considered as rent until completed, (c) monthly payments represented a smaller fraction of the amount due than would have been welcome from the same customer on a charge account, although the total amount due was probably larger than would have been welcome on that customer's charge account, and (d) a "down payment" usually was required.

10. Smock (1962, p. 88) amplifies this important point. Smock's observation on the development of installment credit noted the historical evidence tracing installment bonds in a 1789 advertisement and the fact that consumer credit was utilized in English cities during the mid nineteenth century.

11. Smock (1962, p. 91) notes that installment sales were instrumental in permitting the purchase of both expensive consumer durables and everyday commodities. The advent of installment plans accompanying the Singer Sewing Machine is also noted. Smock (1962) reinforces Bourdieu's (1984) point on the impact of social status (or habitus):

Installment sales were confined almost universally to goods which had a satisfactory resale market; terms of repayment appear to have been relatively short and down-payments substantial; and installment credit privileges appear to have been limited to persons who enjoyed good credit reputations and who were well able to meet their contracts.

12. Bass (1977) expands on detail supplied by Johnson (1970) and Smock (1962). She reports that:

The practice of buying durable goods on time goes back more than a hundred years. The rudiments of modern installment retailing were already present in 1856 when Isaac Singer found that he could sell many more sewing machines by financing their purchase. In one year after he introduced the idea of hire purchase (installment financing) his sewing machine sales had tripled.

13. Bass (1977, p.108) expanded on the significance of the transition from primitive credit plans into the everyday acceptance of consumer or retail credit. Installment credit practices had spread throughout most of the eastern states by the turn of the century. The convenience and prestige for relatively wealthy consumers were shared with normal consumers.

14. Bass (1977) cites the retail industry feeling about consumer credit prior to 1911:

Prior to 1911, the generally accepted thinking of the era was to discourage "time buying." Such stalwarts as Sears, Roebuck and Co. published admonitory editorials in their mail order catalogues advising customers not to be misled by firms advertising time payments.

15. Bass (1977, p. 107) notes that the invention of installment credit and extension into everyday consumer transactions since World War II created a more receptive and tolerant stance toward installment buying.

16. "Democratization of Consumer Credit" was a working concept originally suggested by the late Joseph Bensman in 1983 during the early developmental stages of the study.

17. Bass offers the following concise development of this process. The first wave of installment buying occurred World War I with the introduction of consumer durables and creation of installment selling. Consumers generally utilize numerous appliance and other services that total at least $5,000 to $10,000.

18. Dauten (1956, p.11) is quoted as claiming that industrialization and mass production accompanied the development of marketplace demand. The mass market was created through increasing incomes and changing modes of living.

19. Bass (1977) claimed that they (the retailers) were discouraged by "the prevailing low standards of the credit industry and they were apprehensive about promoting instalment credit because of their customers' negative reactions to it, but most of all they had not yet realized its potential as a merchandising device" (p. 110).

20. Bass noted the following in her analysis of the consumer credit boom. Retail stores started offering retail buying once the public accepted that the practice did not carry personal stigma. The era following World War II could fully capitalize on the economic practice.

21. Refer to Bourdieu's (1984) synthesis of a grand theory indicating the power of social forces binding together structural units. The later theoretical posturing of Giddens (1987) and other theorists on structuralism (combining geographical location with an existing time frame or sociospatial formation) builds on these ideas. Zukin and DiMaggio (1990) and other political economic analysts also draw on these seminal ideas.

22. Subsequent material will document how this technological development greatly influenced the expansion of the retail industry.

23. The so called Fordist era featured mass production for the purpose of supplying a standardized product while the post-Fordist period ostensibly emphasized niche marketing in many diversified consumer domains. Piore and Sable (1984) cover this transformation within a larger economic discussion of the technostructure.

24. Neal (1967, pp. 152–153) summarized the development of revolving accounts.

25. The reader must note that the following material describes the economic state of department store operations in the late 1970s. A fuller consideration of where the department store industry stands after the 1980s will follow in a later section.

26. Several of these department stores or corporate retailing firms are either out of business or consolidated with other corporations. For example, Federated,

Dayton-Hudson, and Gimbel's filed for bankruptcy and have subsequently closed in recent years.

27. The list is somewhat out of date but provides a good idea of the potential profitability in the retail sector.

28. Sears and J. C. Penney have nationwide customers through their catalog divisions, while Woolworth and several other stores offer general merchandise fulfilling everyday consumer needs.

29. Leveraged buyouts (LBOs) are economic transactions wherein one company acquires another and sells off portions of the acquired property in satisfying the huge debt. Campeau, Inc. acquired the Allied and Federated retailing chains (stores acquired included Bloomingdale's, Stern's, Abraham and Straus, and other leading retailers). Several of these stores were sold, and others went into temporary bankruptcy protection to shield the parent company and satisfy the large debt.

30. Jacobs cites the *Wall Street Journal*, April 21, 1982, as his source of information on shopping center growth.

31. The concept of mall development and the transformation of retailing into a theme park phenomenon was discussed by Rybczynski, 1993.

32. Piore and Sable (1984) argued that industrial production was guided by the advent of flexible specialization or the extension of the manufacturing sector into the production of varied consumer goods. Harvey (1989) and others argue that the process is a reflection of post Fordist tendencies within the capitalist system.

33. Retail marketing, as discussed in the next section, does have its limits. The reader should realize that frequent recessionary times are a reflection of the cultural and economic bases of retail credit. According to a published account five years ago in the *New York Times* (1992, p. D1), 47th Street Photo joined Newmark and Lewis, another electronics discuount chain, and Seaman's, a leading furniture discount outlet, in filing for bankruptcy under Chapter 11. Stephanie Strom, a *New York Times* reporter, included the following observation about the nature of previous marketing success at 47th Street Photo: 47th Street Photo never expanded but built a lucrative mail order business.

34. Department stores evolved in response to the everyday needs of a consumer population dependent on industrial (or manufacturing) efforts for specific products. The pre-urban consumer was less dependent on manufacturing concerns. Rural-dwelling consumers either self-produced clothing and other goods or purchased necesary items from a general store. A later section in this chapter addresses the evolution of the retail industry.

35. Other examples of boutiques catering to limited consumer interests are available. Meredith Brokaw, wife of network news anchor Tom Brokaw, operates a trendy toy store for people seeking special items. The post-Fordist trend toward narrow interests includes boutique formation in the electronic industry. Cable television offers specific channels appealing to particular audiences. News, country music, nostalgia, entertainment, science fiction, popular music, and religion are just a few interests served through cable channels. Television networks are comparable to department stores. The cable offshoots are symbolic of boutiques serving specialized interests.

36. Discount chains were a lucrative part of the retail industry until the advent of the current recession. See the forthcoming discussion of the present economic state of the retail industry for more substantive information.

37. The phrase "wish list" came into usage with consumer desires (or wishes) to purchase the merchandise listed in omnibus catalogs offering a myriad group of choices.

38. A 1989 documentary airing on the Public Broadcasting Service (PBS) as part of their *American Experience* series chronicles the rise of the Sears catalog business.

39. The American public indicates an interest in acquiring particular consumer goods. The commodities are then produced in fulfilling the indicated marketing demand. In spite of the most sophisticated advertising industry efforts, achieving economic profitability ultimately depends on funneling the produced commodities through accessible retail outlets.

40. Ewen (1988) argues that consumers are seduced by fads or styles. The outside techostructure remained aloof from an everyday discourse dictated by media influence.

41. A superstation is a local station from one region of the country that is carried nationwide via cable systems. Some of these stations include WWOR (Channel 9, New York City), WGN (Channel 9, Chicago), WPIX (Channel 11, New York), and other stations in Boston, San Francisco and major urban markets.

42. Consumers previously ordered via catalogs offered by department stores and specialty companies.

43. Hawk (1988, pp. 26–28) elaborates on these ideas.

44. Agnew (1987, pp. 1,20) reports on the impact of home shopping.

45. See Bourdieu (1984) and other similar analyses for an elaboration on the cultural capital (or poststructural) theme.

6

Consumer Debt and the Social Impact of Credit

The shift from preindustrial to industrial to postindustrial and finally to postmodern (or poststructural) formation was a significant transition from the early twentieth century to the present within the developing American economic system.[1] A constantly changing mode of production shaped consumer wants and needs.[2] The means of production and, most important, marketing appeal shifted as the post-Fordist (or niche marketing) approach took center stage. Niche marketing gave way to nebulous choices and a basic definition of social life based on available choices in material goods, attainable services, and accessible social experiences. The postmodern perspective stressed continual redefinition of everyday needs and constantly changing consumer cultural values.

Consumer acceptance of credit extension and the social desirability of consumer debt was achieved through gradual enculturation. Desires were fulfilled through immediate gratification rather than deferred saving. Consumers strived for the benefits that available goods and services offered in improving their social lives. Household items stood as a form of positional goods for the lower-class cohort.[3] David Caplovitz (1965) pointed out that consumers sought furniture and appliances as an indication of permanence.[4] Tangible things such as furniture or clothing offered an affirmation that individuals accepted particular styles or fashion.

Schor (1998) taps into some of this thinking with an incisive analysis of consumer behavior, consumption, and social class identification. Schor identifies consumer desires for enhanced conspicuous spending (e.g., vacation homes, travel, cars) and the upscaling of these self-identified needs (p.16). Additionally, Schor tells us that the newly emerging necessities include home computers, answer machines, home air conditioning, clothes driers, and automobiles (pp. 16–17).

In effect, Schor borrows from Bourdieu's (1984) emphasis on distinction and social style. Her analysis of upscaling (acquiring more material possessions) and downshifting (cutting back as the income levels fail to provide enough economic comfort) fits the changing consumer roles in the late twentieth century. Her profile of a downshifter includes individuals buying organic fare, repairs rather than buying, reusing recycled paper bags, giving up gym membership to walk with spousal equivalent in the evenings, making own clothes, living for the moment, utilizing local barter systems, and conserving blowdrying energy (p. 112).

Schor's main point is that American consumer behavior is patterned according to affluence depicted in pre-sold media images. The individuals portrayed in television programs and motion pictures embrace a lifestyle supported through pronounced spending. The cultural values contradict American ability to "keep up with the Joneses." The average American in a middle or upper-middle class economic bracket cannot continue carrying heavy debt for long periods of time without experiencing frustration. Struggling with consumer debt and seeing earned income disappear for ongoing credit card bills does have an eventual sobering impact (pp. 14-15).[5]

The relationship between cultural values and economic development (as discussed by Schor) dictated a reorganization of social status (or prestige) The relationship between cultural values and economic development dictated a reorganization of social status (or prestige) guidelines (see Bourdieu, 1984). Debt accumulation (also termed "debt entanglement" by Caplovitz) was now entrenched as an acceptable method of putting on social appearances. An entire generation accepted ongoing debt obligations rather than the traditionally held view that purchases were consummated when funds were immediately available. The overall impact of these events was reflected in the post-Fordist emphasis on diversification rather than standard production procedures (Harvey, 1989). "Present orientation" replaced planning for future consumption among many American consumers. The difference between the economically disadvantaged (or, in Wilson's terminology [1991], "the ghetto poor") and the rising middle class was defined as immediate leisure choices versus necessity. New material and nonmaterial products emerged as the evolving cultural system incor-

porated new status symbols or experiences (e.g., telecharge systems wherein consumers can charge a movie ticket at a reserved time for a popular film attracting major audience attention).[6] Thus, the consumer appeal of visiting a theme park (or telling friends and coworkers about one's experience—along with generating photographs) becomes a culturally approved social activity.[7]

Additionally, the perceptible shift in credit card advertising emphasized intangible or nonmaterial experience or the growth of the theme park and tourist industries. These activities were dependent upon and facilitated by credit card purchasing as an enabling factor. Marketing strategy categorized by "buy now, pay later" was replaced with a cautious economic rationale.[8] That contradictory rationale lasted while consumers found themselves visibly coping with debt accumulated during the later stages of the 1980s. The debt was created through credit cards and other devices helping to facilitate immediate attainment of certain experiences perceived as wants but transformed into cultural needs. The advertised products were made available through an ever-evolving retail system linked with social changes in residential location, consumer employment location, and advanced telecommunications technology.

This chapter completes the progression of events described above and detailed in previous sections. More significantly, the impact of consumer credit is a serious concern in the unfolding of more complex social choices. The industrial sector is caught amidst a serious set of circumstances. On the one hand, manufacturers and distributors are eager for an ever expanding consumer business. Alternately, how long can consumers continue spending before their accumulated obligations are beyond practical financi' means? How can an ideology associated with consumer culture adjus' apparent prosperity in everyday consumer lives? Are there any limits ' ciated with contingencies wherein consumer debt levels develop intr sonal problem? What about the declining significance of bankrup' expanding economy?

Forthcoming discussion centers around the importance within the federal bankruptcy laws during the late 1970s. T tem finally acknowledged that bankruptcy did not carry f stigma it once did, and there was a significant increase in ing with consumer debt. Consumers can apply for d' keep most of their possessions. Ironically, consumer come good credit risks for banks and other financia' in expanding a base of potential credit card custom ers declaring bankruptcy cannot apply for simil' seven years.

Information on the importance of consumer debt is incorporated in providing meaningful conclusions about consumer spending and its social significance. Consideration of cultural changes in the discussion of consumer credit incorporates an examination of socio-historical regulative initiatives. What is the impact of the Equal Credit Opportunity Act and revamped bankruptcy laws as derived from a lenient cultural system stressing debtor forgiveness? Lastly, what are the repercussions of economic control and impending cultural values?

DEBT AND THE EXPANSION OF CONSUMER CREDIT

A more extensive examination of consumer credit growth and its implications facilitates the understanding of increased bankruptcy rates and a subsequent reinterpretation of bankruptcy from a postmodern perspective. Bankruptcy does not carry the same social stigma as it did during the pre-1978 period. Revision of the Federal Bankruptcy Laws allowing a more lenient attitude toward consumer default did not occur until 1978. Altered consumer perceptions regarding debt acceptance produced liberalized changes in the bankruptcy laws, accompanied by massive consumer debt expansion during the 1980s and the realization that continued spending facilitates post-Fordist tendencies (allowing distribution of more differentiated products). In a postmodern sense, the image of bankruptcy (or overwhelming debt accumulation) as a negative character flaw was reconceptualized as a temporary condition.

The rise of consumer debt and a transformation in social attitudes toward debt are major elements in the development of new social definitions surrounding bankruptcy status. An increased consumer acceptance of consumer credit and rising debt levels contributed to more pronounced debt levels. According to Philip Klein (1971)[9], consumer credit use spread at a phenomenal rate in the period between 1920 and 1967. Klein claimed that consumer credit growth was concentrated in three periods. The first period occurred in the 1920s, peaking in 1929. The second period extended from the Great Depression until 1941. The third period began at the end of World War II and continues. Klein claims that consumer credit has more than quadrupled since 1950—increasing from about $20 billion to almost $100 billion in 1967.

Families in 1946 were adjusting economically to the impact of World War II. Stringent controls on the production of consumer goods prevented any pronounced buying activity. Consumer installment debt outstanding at the end of 1945 was only $2.5 billion. As Luckett (1988, pp. 591–603) observes, total was equivalent to about $16 billion in 1987 dollars.

Federal Reserve statistics elaborate on consumer credit levels and trends income, spending, and savings rates. The economic measures are impor-

tant because the creation of surplus goods and new consumer products is directly influenced by consumer demand and available cash or credit resources. The pattern of growth in total outstanding installment credit in the period from 1929 to 1967 is particularly interesting. Federal Reserve System statistics indicate $35.1 million in outstanding installment credit in 1929, $17.8 million in 1933, $72.6 million in 1941, $24.3 million in 1944, and progressively higher volume throughout the post–World War II period from 1945 to 1967 ($25.8 million in 1945 and $901.8 million in 1967) (P. Klein, 1971, pp. 73–74). The cyclical pattern indicates that consumer credit use was relatively high in 1929 (the first year of the Great Depression). Many analysts blame the overextension of consumer credit for the depression conditions during 1929 to the early 1940s. The United States began a brief climb out of the depression in 1941, consumer activity slackened due to scarce consumer goods, and consumer credit volume really picked up from the mid 1940s until the late 1960s (pp. 73–74).

The heavy use of credit cards and other forms of consumer installment credit extended into the 1980s. Total personal income totaled $4.1 billion in 1988. Americans were also spending a significant percentage of their earned income. Disposable personal income was $3.5 billion, personal outlays were $3.3 billion, and personal savings was $143.6 million. The overall savings rate fluctuated from 4.4 percent in 1985 and early 1986 to a low of approximately 2.3 percent during the third quarter of 1987 (*Federal Reserve Bulletin*, 1989, p. A54).[10]

Credit card distribution increased by major proportions during the period from the 1970s to the mid-1980s. Mandell (1990, p. 153) noted the widespread acceptance of consumer credit cards. According to his analysis, the growth of consumer credit was conspicuous as 1984 statistics revealed that 71 percent of all families acquired a credit card. The bankcard industry reflected a significant increase in consumer credit expansion. The period between 1970 and 1986 featured a pronounced increase from 16 to 55 percent of families owning a bankcard. Sixty two percent of the consumers possessed a retail card, and 34 percent carried a gas card. Visa was the most popular card: 43 percent of all Americans between 17 and 65 carried the card. The nearest leading competitors were Sears (38.4 percent) and Mastercard (30.1 percent). According to Mandell, the leading gas cards were Amoco (13.9 percent) and Shell (9.5 percent). American Express led in charge volume with $74.3 billion, followed by Citibank ($19.5 billion) and Sears ($13.4 billion). Citibank led in outstanding debt ($15 billion) by a close margin over American Express and Sears (p. 153).

Consumer debt generated by credit card use emerged as a major factor in the development of the consumer credit business. Credit cards were a significant element in facilitating increased consumer spending during the

1970s and the 1980s. Previous sections discussed the relationship between credit cards and the convenience of immediate consumer spending. The ascendance of the consumer culture and emphasis on immediate gratification produced an important social economic change: thrift was deemphasized and consumption became the social norm. According to Mandell, the credit card industry exerted a significant impact on consumer debt. Mandell cites a study by Glenn Canner that revealed that the proportion of credit card owners using revolving credit during 1970–1986 remained constant at 50 percent. However, the average outstanding balance doubled from $649 in 1970 to $1,472 in 1986. Further, 1983 consumer credit debt accounted for 16.9 percent of total installment payments. Not coincidentally, the proportion of consumer debt to disposable personal income increased from 14 percent in 1982 to 18 percent in 1986 (p. 79).

Basic changes in the credit card industry led to more potential consumer payment default on credit card accounts and contributed to bankruptcy rates. Mandell addressed consumer default on credit card balances and the impact of heightened industrial competition. He claimed that increased competition from Discover, Optima, and affinity cards eroded the profitability of bankcard business operations. As a result, many banks accepted customers with lower credit ratings. The ultimate result was that the marginal accounts with higher balances produced an increase in net charge offs. Consequently, charge-offs in the United States doubled from 1.5 percent in 1984 to 3.2 percent in 1986. The Nilson Report indicated that worldwide charge off rates were 4.01 percent in 1987 (p. 89).

Overall consumer credit levels increased dramatically during the 1980s. Consumer credit reached $655 billion by September 1988. According to the Federal Reserve Board, debt distribution was distributed as follows: commercial banks, $308.8 billion; finance companies, $142.7 billion; credit unions, $86.7 billion; retailers, $39.3 billion; savings institutions, $43.9 billion; and gasoline companies, $3.6 billion (*Federal Reserve Bulletin*, 1989, p. A54). Credit card debt was responsible for approximately 4 percent of the total credit outlays. However, credit card profit matched and exceeded the economic advantages of automobile loans, mortgages, and ordinary loans. Bank funds for credit card lines of credit were borrowed for approximately 3 to 4 percent and loaned to consumers at rates ranging from 11 to 21 percent (Mandell, 1991, p. 153).[11]

GROWTH OF THE BANKRUPTCY PHENOMENON

Statistics only convey part of the story. The previously detailed statistics provide a snapshot of economic activity and growth of consumer installment credit. Rampant acceptance of consumer credit created higher levels of consumer debt during the 1980s. Luckett (1988, pp. 591–603) documented the trend toward pervasive consumer activity. Revisions in bankruptcy laws were instrumental in furthering the expansion of consumer debt. Luckett points out that personal bankruptcy filings in 1946 totaled fewer than 9,000. As a comparative measure, 9,000 bankruptcies per week were the norm in 1988.

A combination of recessionary periods and legislative changes was responsible for heightened bankruptcy rates. Bankruptcies rose each year from 1946 until the mid-1960s. Consumer bankruptcy rates hit a high of 190,000 cases in 1967. Historical trends then indicate a fluctuation in bankruptcy rates from 1968 to 1980. High inflation during the 1970s pushed many more people into filing for bankruptcy.

As Luckett notes, personal bankruptcies increased throughout much of the 1980s. Back to back recessions during the early 1980s brought the unemployment rate from less than 6 percent to more than 10 percent. The higher unemployment rate was accompanied by a major revision to federal bankruptcy laws during fall 1979. Bankruptcy became more attractive to debtors because the liberalized law increased the amount of assets exempt from liquidation.

Bankruptcies jumped from about 200,000 cases in 1979 to nearly 315,000 in 1982. Bankruptcies declined during 1983 and 1984 but increased during 1985 and 1986, with a 205 percent increase during each year. Bankruptcy rates slowed in the following years, but the number of bankruptcy cases filed totaled nearly 500,000.

Luckett's information was amplified by Cocheo (1991). According to Cocheo, bankruptcy filings for the year ending June 1990 totaled 660,796 cases. The 1990 bankruptcy incidence was a nearly 14 percent increase from the previous year (pp. 443–46).

These numbers illustrate that bankruptcy surfaced as a viable social choice during the mid 1980s. But how do we explain the significance of the social economic transformation from social stigma to an accepted administrative procedure? Some of the answers are developed by Sullivan, Warren, and Westbrook (1989) in their groundbreaking study of bankruptcy and consumer credit in America. The authors examine legal remedies facilitating bankruptcy through Chapters 7 and 13 of the 1978 Bankruptcy Code. Their analysis incorporates an analysis of bankruptcy law as a social remedy for serious debt problems and creditors.

Several questions frame their examination of bankruptcy as a serious social issue. The three central questions raised by the authors are the following: Who are the debtors and the creditors in bankruptcy? What factors have contributed to the spectacular increases in consumer bankruptcy? and how should these data affect the normative and policy decisions underlying consumer bankruptcy laws? Their subsequent analysis considers specific circumstances (layoffs, medical debts, low incomes, business failures, and credit junkies) wherein bankruptcy occurs.

Key issues emerge in an analysis surrounding post-Fordism, the postmodern dilemma of contradictory positive and negative connotations surrounding consumer debt, and the cultural changes as fueled by economic reform. Sullivan and coauthors explained the following contradiction: Consumer bankruptcy acted as an "economic and social safety valve" permitting debtors to survive in an economic system that needed continued consumer support to exist (p. 8).

The contradiction implied in the preceding paragraph is equally social, financial and moral. The moral dimension developed by Sullivan, Warren, and Westbrook indicates an ongoing ambivalence about bankruptcy. The cultural values inbred within American society emphasize celebrity status through hard work and achievement. Our society admires people who undertake comebacks in the midst of adversity. Emphasis is placed on the celebration of people as distinguished by social credentials earned by accumulating material possessions and myriad travel experiences.

Cultural appropriation of success as a desired social status is operative in defining social acceptance. Fault is measured in terms of desirable social character (i.e., the admired work ethic) and violations of the success stereotype. Thus, Sullivan and colleagues state that we favor the unemployed steelworker over the "grasshopper hedonist." How can we account for the operative procedure responsible for assigning fault or blame? Is debtor victimization precipitated by the limitless promise of profits in a post Fordist economic setting? After all, we can blame the bank or finance company for offering the initial loan or credit line regardless of whether the consumer can meet his or her subsequent obligations.

THE DECLINING SIGNIFICANCE OF BANKRUPTCY

The relative social acceptance of bankruptcy did not always carry such benign meaning. There was a time when consumer debt was viewed with disapproval by most people. Social attitudes changed when middle- and working-class families, since the 1920s, began relying on relatively high installment credit payments on borrowed funds. The resulting consequences and reluctant shift toward the cultural acceptance of "starting over with a clean slate" were an integral part of the capitalist system.[12]

A consideration of how the cultural contradictions built within capitalism produce such ambivalent feelings reveals the nature of current social attitudes toward bankruptcy. According to Daniel Bell (1976b, pp. 64-65), the rise of urban settings contributed to the erosion of traditional religious values. He claimed that the American social structure was transformed with the rise of urban centers. Additionally, the consumption society emerged with an emphasis on spending and materialist values. The new system undermined the traditional value system stressing "thrift, frugality, self control, and impulse renunciation." A simultaneous technological revolution highlighted by automobiles, motion pictures, and radio encouraged cultural homogeneity. According to Bell, this social transformation was responsible for the end of puritanism as a set of practices that could support the traditional value system (p. 76).

Bell traced the relationship between mass consumption and consumer cultural alterations in everyday life. Bell provided an important analysis of "the transparent life" pp. 65-66). The cultural transformation within modern society is attributable to past luxuries accepted as necessities. Changes in household technology and the spread of installment buying undermined Protestant fear of debt. The creation of a common culture facilitated by transportation and communications intensified a desire for consumer credit.[13]

The developing consumer culture accompanied a significant change in social values. Bell again concisely states the nature of social economic change within everyday lifestyles:[14]

All this [advertising and rapid social change] came about by gearing society to change and the acceptance of cultural change, once mass consumption and a high standard of living were seen as the legitimate purpose of economic organization. Selling became the most striking activity of contemporary America. Against frugality, selling emphasized prodigality; against asceticism, the lavish display. (p. 69)

The inherent cultural contradictions encouraging the creation of consumer debt come to the forefront in Bell's analysis of consumer spending, creation of consumer debt, and the Protestant ethic (p. 69). Bell points out that saving and abstinence are integral parts of the Protestant ethic. Bell also offers an insightful view of consumer debt and social structure within a more elaborate discussion of hedonism and shift in American values (pp.69–70).[15]

The cultural contradictions between work and the encouragement of consumption are basic themes in Bell's discussion (pp. 71, 75). Bell wrote that there was a "disjuncture between the norms of culture and social structure and a contradiction between the social structure itself." The contradiction stemmed from the reinforced corporate work ethic and the consumption of pleasure and self-gratification (pp. 70–71).

Bell offers an interesting interpretation of how the disjunction produced through a change in social values impacted on contemporary society and the shift into idealizing the middle-class standard of living. The "new capitalism" stressed production in the workplace and a contradictory emphasis on leisure consumption (p. 75).

Bell's discussion of the disjuncture between the puritan value system and the coming of the consumer society emphasized significant changes surrounding the consumer culture. The emergent emphasis on a higher standard of living, increased consumption, and the promotion of material or nonmaterial (symbolic) goods accompanied the creation of surplus goods and new consumer products.[16]

Bell's distinction between traditional thrift values and the emergent consumer culture carries important implications. The emergent consumer society featured a culture dependent on increased consumption. Debt becomes an important mainstay in both the consumer culture and everyday economic activity. Mandell (1990) discussed the dependence between these two factors. Willing consumer spending enabled the expansion of merchant enterprises. Mandell notes that the credit card industry fit the needs of a mobile, affluent society. The credit card enabled a more widespread and universal consumer culture (pp. 153–154).

The credit card flourished and, as previously discussed, so did the increase in consumer default and bankruptcy rates. Consumer credit was increasingly democratized as merchants needed to overcome a zero-sum growth in consumers interested in holding and using credit cards. Therefore, greater credit risks (consumers with recorded bankruptcy filings, lower- and middle-income consumers with high debt obligations, college students) were offered credit card privileges.

The growth of the consumer credit system and distribution of goods, services, and everyday social experience (theme parks, vacation excursions) was dependent on maintaining a high volume of active consumer transactions. The reconfiguration of bankruptcy as an intermediate stage, rather than a final social economic denigration, and the impact of consumer credit upon quality of life form the last facets of the overall analysis presented in this study.

BANKRUPTCY AND THE IMPACT OF THE LEGAL SYSTEM

Consumer bankruptcy evolved from an undesirable social practice into a "business-as-usual" measure employed by debt-ridden individuals. Citizens often find themselves in "over their heads" as an inevitable result of a consumer culture encouraging immediate commodity acquisition. Debt is a necessary component within the lives of most people. We are always utilizing the convenience afforded by credit card installment debt. With the spread of credit card acceptance throughout the economic sector, people can facilitate the immediate acquisition of food, clothing, and other forms of immediate needs (e.g., admissions to theme parks or charging airline tickets).

A postmodern perspective on consumer debt would state that lenient attitudes toward bankruptcy reflect a change in societal feelings about accumulated debt. The creation of an immediate problem (consumer debt) is justified with the rationale that consumer cultural values justify the emphasis on consumption. Objects signifying cultural capital are transformed into economic capital. The desire for consumer goods stems from a striving for better living accommodations, a more cultured background obtained through travel, certain health or other culinary tastes, and exposure to mass culture. The consumption of images (or cultural capital) and its transformation into economic capital (or monetary value ensuring a commercial profit) support the business sector and intensify the spread of consumer culture. The marketing of cultural symbols or taste (which Bourdieu [1984], refers to as "habitus") is associated with a given product. The social values, or positioning, justifies consumer expenditure for the product, regardless of the overall cost.[17]

This above analysis of consumer debt incorporates an understanding of the legal changes facilitating lessened social stigma associated with bankruptcy and immediate reestablishment of consumer credit entitlement. Bankruptcy is a legal position associated with social and economic consequences. An understanding of the process entails knowing the types of bankruptcy protection and how changes in the laws reflect the evolvement of consumer debt.

More than 400,000 American consumers filed for bankruptcy in 1986. The number has more than doubled in less than a decade. It is useful to distinguish two types of bankruptcy categories: Chapter 7 and Chapter 13. Debtors choosing Chapter 7 give up all assets not legally sheltered from creditor seizure. In return, debtors receive a discharge or legal release from most preexisting debts. Proceeds from the sale of the seized objects are sold or liquidated and distributed among the creditors. Some celebrities that faced this situation include singer Willie Nelson and the late comedian Redd Foxx (see Sullivan, Warren, and Westbrook, 1989).

Chapter 13 of the Bankruptcy Code allows debtors to keep all property in exchange for negotiated debt payment agreement. Instead of liquidation, consumers must make a debt settlement over a set time period. Chapter 13 is viable only when invoked by an individual with modest debts (secured debts below $350,000 or unsecured debts over $100,000).

The liberalized federal bankruptcy laws had a distinctive effect on recorded bankruptcy rates. There were 0.07 bankruptcies per 1,000 persons in 1945; the number rose to 0.88 in 1965; 0.92 in 1970; and 1.07 in 1975. With the effective implementation of the new Federal Bankruptcy Law in 1980, the number rose to 1.25 bankruptcies per 1,000 persons. There was a considerable increase between 1980 and 1987. Some 2.03 bankruptcies per 1,000 persons were recorded in 1987 (Luckett, 1988). The debt-to-income ratio was also rising during the same time period. There was a 1.7 percent debt-to-income ratio in 1945; the number rose to 15 percent in 1965, declined to 14.6 percent during the mid 1970s recession, rose to 15.5 percent in 1980, and eventually increased to 19.3 percent in 1987 (p. 595).

Luckett presents American Bankers Association data supporting the impact of bankcard credit debt. Losses not recovered by creditors as a percentage of credit outstanding during 1983–1986 ranged from 1.27 percent in 1984 to 1.40 in 1986. Percentage of losses due to bankruptcy ranged from 25.2 percent in 1984 to 32.7 percent in 1986. Finally, losses due to bankruptcy as a percent of credit outstanding were recorded at 0.34 in 1983, 0.32 in 1984, 0.51 in 1985, and 0.46 in 1986. However, bankcard credit losses ranged from 1.09 percent in 1984 to a high of 2.35 percent in 1980. The percentage was 2.23 percent in 1986 (p. 598).

Credit card debt was forgivable because financial institutions still made a profit on consumer transactions. The imposition of annual fees, relatively high interest rates in proportion to federal Reserve money rates, and the marketing of subsidiary services guaranteed a profit against charge-offs. Some consumers still managed to find themselves facing substantial debt. The sample of Texas bankruptcy cases compiled by Sullivan and coworkers (1989, p.183) averaged $3,741 in total credit card debt, $2,010 in all purpose credit card debt, and $2,933 in store credit card debt.

But consumer debt keeps rising, more debt and bankruptcies are encouraged by the business community, and the economic system functions at a normal pace. A certain form of "social control," as created by the social economic system, seems to explain the development of rising consumer debt and pronounced economic activity. The purchase of products and marketed experience, as facilitated by credit card use, is legitimated by vesting consumer culture with cultural capital. The business community and government agencies regulating economic growth desire consumer activity. The consumer credit system, comprising the advertising, marketing, and distribution of credit cards and consumer goods, depends on sufficient business volume. Thus, financial institutions offering credit cards and department stores selling merchandise continually promote their products. At the same time, the business community does not desire massive bankruptcies to the extent that consumers are no longer viable customers. Bell (1976b) identifies this general trend between thrift and spending as one of the important cultural contradictions in capitalism (see Bell for more information).

Television credit card commercials typify an ongoing contradiction in the economy. Depending on the number of consumer bankruptcies and government pressure on consumer credit as an inflationary factor, credit card commercials will emphasize either conspicuous consumption (in the case of ongoing Visa advertisements featuring tropical or exotic locations) or, in the case of current Mastercard advertisements, ordinary uses for the bank credit card.

Therefore, the legal system adjusted the bankruptcy laws in an effort to identify prolific consumers facing major indebtedness. A major contradiction does exist at this point. The postmodern image of consumer credit and consumer culture dominates American society. There is no escape from consumer debt in a society based on the establishment of economic capital emanating from products associated with cultural symbols or masterfully marketed utility for the lives of consumers.

The penalty for invoking bankruptcy protection seems somewhat irrelevant at times. Consumers will voluntarily cut up their credit cards ("plastic surgery") and repay a portion of their debts. In the meantime, consumers are reoffered bank credit cards, secured credit cards (credit cards with a balance based on the amount of a security payment), and department store accounts. Creditors know that the consumer cannot apply for bankruptcy protection for another seven years. According to Sullivan, Warren, and Westbrook (1989), most consumers file for bankruptcy protection only once in their lives.

Debt and the consumer culture also conspicuously affects particular segments. Bankcard issuers went after new population groups after exhausting the number of working men interested in owning a credit card. Women were targeted in the 1970s and college students (where recruiters visit campuses, offering limited credit line accounts) during the past decade. In the case of women, passage of the Equal Credit Opportunity Act in 1970 provided that women would be entitled to credit in their own name. However, Sullivan and coworkers comment that there are insufficient data showing the exact increase in women filing for bankruptcy protection. Most instances occur among single women and married women discovering that two incomes no longer support a family (p. 197).

The process of declaring bankruptcy is the end of an intricate and calculated economic process. The final chapter examines the overall implications of consumer credit and offers a prognosis for the future.

NOTES

1. See the previous discussion in Chapters 1 and 2. Additionally, Bell (1976a) contributes an important statement linking the industrial, postindustrial and postmodern viewpoints.

2. Bell (1976b) indicates how the postindustrial society emphasized a service sector affording enhanced leisure time. Bell's sense of contradiction stemmed

from the values placed on work versus the push for consumer spending incentives.

3. Refer to Hirsch's 1974 discussion of positional goods.

4. Caplovitz (1965) claimed that the poverty stricken or lower income population sought affirmation that they had tangible roots in the community. He argued that substandard furniture and appliances bought on installment credit plans had an intrinsic symbolic value beyond a utilitarian household function.

Schor (1998) brings together information on consumer spending, social status change, and American consumer reappraisal of their expenditures in relation with lifestyle choices.

5. Bourdieu (1984) points out that social status and cultural values are closely intertwined in a society dependent on continually redefining normative social appearance.

6. Many social critics miss the essential point behind the sociocultural influences associated with theme parks. Some theorists (especially Zukin, 1991) insist on equating theme parks with representational power (or cultural appropriation). The forced determinist analysis of economic and cultural forces clearly neglects and negates an empirically based understanding of socio-cultural forces. Refer to Featherstone (1991) and MacCannell (1991) for a more comprehensive view of tourism and consumer culture.

7. A leading advertising executive provided some information during the course of a telephone conversation. A shift between impulsive consumption and careful choice based on everyday lifestyles occurred within the last decade. Adam Smith, on a PBS program (See Public Broadcasting Service, 1992) pointed out that MasterCard's message during the 1980s was "Master the possibilities." Celebrities were promoting active consumption. The more recent message during the 1990s emphasizes consumer savings and the practical applications afforded by using MasterCard. The previous chapter on advertising detailed the essence of this shift.

8. Klein, 1971, Page 4, accepts the Federal Reserve Board definition of consumer credit: "Consumer credit includes short- and intermediate-term credit that is extended through regular business channels to finance the purchase of commodities, and services for personal consumption, or to refinance debts incurred for such purposes" (p. 4).

9. The statistics presented document economic activity, consumer earnings and expenditures, overall levels of consumer credit activity, and consumer personal savings resources.

10. The spread betrween the cost of borrowing money and interest rates charged consumers, generation of annual fees on credit cards, and higher late penalties transformed credit cards into a very successful and lucrative financial instrument.

11. Max Weber's discussion of the Protestant ethic emphasized the religious doctrine against extending oneself beyond one's immediate financial means and paying "high usury rates." The original domination of nineteenth-century American society by such influences and the ascendance of secular (or materialist) values during the twentieth century are more fully discussed in Weber (1902/1958).

12. Bell accounts for the creation of consumer culture. Bell relates mass consumption with social habits and the impact of social invention. One could argue

that the advent of installment credit legitimized the introduction of credit cards as a significant social invention in this elaboration of secular values.

13. Bell summarized the importance of consumer credit and the overall impact of consumer debt on the lives of American families. Bell claimed that installment debt triggered major social changes. Originally, installment selling carried "two stigmas." First, most installment debt was incurred by the poor in the process of dealing with peddlers making weekly connections. Therefore, installment selling was viewed as an indication of financial instability. Second, installment debt meant that the middle class was engaging in a practice construed as "wrong and dangerous." One could not be perceived as living beyond their means. The thinking was that people should save for major purchases. Industrious and thrifty behavior was socially acceptable. Consumer credit could thrive only when "debt" was replaced by "credit," and the purchasers were discretely billed through the mail.

14. Bell offers the following analysis. The acceptance of consumer credit was tied to a shift in the so-called Protestant ethic wherein people were allowed to overdraw funds. Bell further elaborated on the notion of social status, culture, and consumer debt. The reinforced relationship between status, taste, and social achievement had shifted. American society went from an emphasis on the virtue of achievement to an emphasis on status and taste. Cultural achievement was symbolized by how to spend and enjoy one's life. Therefore Bell claims that: "the fact was that by the 1950s American culture had become primarily hedonistic, concerned with play, fun, display, and pleasure; and, typical of things in America, in a compulsive way (1976a, p.70).

15. Potter discusses the impact of economic abundance and a freer consumer attitude toward spending as an important social economic change in American society. In addition, niche marketing becomes a potent force as new products are created for select segments of an everexpanding consumer sector. The post-Fordist ideology is gradually transformed into a postmodern setting wherein people consume symbolic goods (or symbols) as viable consumer products. The overall mechanism contributes toward an increase in acceptable consumer debt, a more active lifestyle, and pronounced reliance on consumer credit with resultant debt problems among many societal members (see Sullivan, Warren, and Westbrook, 1989).

16. Cultural capital was discussed within other contexts throughout the study. The best statements on the transition between cultural capital (or symbolic capital) and economic value are rendered by Featherstone (1990); Zukin (1990); Urry (1990); and Bourdieu (1984).

17. Another well-known strategy involves filing for Chapter 11. Chapter 11 is generally used by corporations and partnerships for business reorganizations but is applicable to individuals. Chapter 11 is considered a more desirable repayment plan than Chapter 13 because the debt settlement is lessened. Luckett (1988) provided a comprehensive explanation of the Bankruptcy Reform Act of 1978. The US bankruptcy code originally contained five chapters. Chapter 9 applied to governmental entities. Chapter 7 applied to straight bankruptcy and liquidation of asserts, while Chapter 13 created full or partial repayment of accrued debt. Chapter 12 cases mostly pertained to family farmers.

7

Implications of the Credit Card Society

We are left with a number of important questions. The credit card society is definitely a permanent fixture in the continuing emphasis on consumer behavior. Our final task is to analyze the ultimate meaning of consumerism within the development of postmodern society and some of the latest developments in consumer borrowing and credit card issuance. Credit systems are an easy way to maintain a present orientation encouraging the instant consumption of goods and services. American society offers more choices than in the past. The newly minted goods and services are immediately affordable through credit cards enabling us to "buy now and pay later."

The above conundrum takes on economic and cultural contexts. The 1992 presidential election featured repeated references to the national economy as a "credit card managed system based on perpetual deficits." The 1996 presidential election campaign privoted on the same budgetary issues. Recent discussion about the US government and the mounting federal deficit reduces the problem to a practical concern. How much debt can a government carry and still maintain a basic level of services? The same question can be asked about mounting bankruptcy rates and consumers always struggling to meet their monthly obligations and still allocate sometimes scarce funds for goods, services and leisure experiences.

Consumer credit card issuers continually ask the same question. The recent growth of consumer credit card spending is accompanied by a rise in charge offs (or write offs of uncollectable consumer credit debts) (*New York Times*, 1996a). At the same time, affinity cards are more commonplace among issuers in the professional organizations, nonprofit corporations, charities, and even diverse groups like political parties. Enticements including altruistic support for a popular organization or the accumulation of points for merchandise expand the marketing appeal.

There is some trouble in paradise. Some affinity cards find profits limited through consumers avoiding finance charges by paying monthly credit balances. The General Electric affinity card was quietly charging fees even when consumers paid the entire outstanding balance. The backlash may hurt the future of the GE card and jeopardize other companies considering implementation of the same policies (*New York Times*, 1996a, p. D3).

Other affinity cards are thriving in this competitive atmosphere. The American Express Company introduced a general membership rewards program. Accrued points are redeemable for merchandise. The affinity program costs an additional $50 a year but adds more incentive for consumer spending with the American Express card. According to a *New York Times* report (1996b, p. D4), the Advanta Corporation introduced a credit card that will be linked to the American Express Company's membership rewards program.

The new arrangement is not unlike affinity card programs wherein airlines link up with various bankcard MasterCard or Visa programs in rewarding points toward future air travel. Under the Advanta program, the new no fee credit card, called the rewards accelerator card, will assist American Express cardholders already enrolled in the current membership rewards program. The cardholders can utilize the new Advanta National Bank card as a MasterCard or Visa credit card with an 8.9 percent rate for the first six months. Those customers will earn one point for each $10 of their monthly balance. The American Express Company claims that this arrangement is their first joint venture with another card issuer in the United states (P.D4).

In addition, credit card companies are conceding approximately $0.5 billion in annual credit card debt deemed uncollectable. Clerical incompetence when point-of-sale workers disregard obvious discrepancies between credit cards and customers (even when card photos or signatures differ visibly) intensify the problem.[1]

Other new trends seem equally (if not temporally) foreboding. The Federal Reserve released data indicating that consumer spending is leveling off. According to their September 1996 statistics, borrowers in September 1996 paid off more credit card and other nonmortgage debt than they newly borrowed. Additionally, installment loans declined 2.7 percent at an annual rate. The figures are the lowest in more than three years. In comparison, annual rates of change in previous months indicated consumer borrowing up in previous months—7.4 percent in June, 12.2 percent in July, and 5.2 percent in August. The economy has slowed two thirds since the summer growth (*New York Times*, 1993b, p. D4). Economists point out that the trend is seasonal and expect a rise in consumer spending during the holiday season.

Other trends indicated that automobile debt declined 3.1 percent, and another category including education, mobile homes, vacations, and boats declined 9.1 percent. A last category, revolving debt, increased at a 2.6 percent rate after growing 6.6 percent in August and 18.9 percent in July 1996. The Federal Reserve report points out that consumers were drawing back, although recent statistics are somewhat misleading because of the increasing use of credit cards as convenience or linkage with frequent flyer miles and other benefits. A senior vice president at Visa USA was quoted as saying that 60 percent of card users now pay their entire balance within 30 days, up from 50 percent five years ago. The overall growth of installment debt peaked at 15 percent in July 1995 and recently eased to 9 percent (p. D4).

In a related item, defaults on credit cards and consumer loans rose in September 1996. Tightened controls by lenders and improving wages loosened the overall default rate. Moody's Investor Services Inc. indicated that the charge-off rate (or the percentage of total loans written off as uncollectible) rose to 5.59 percent in September, an increase from 4.27 percent in September 1995. The figure is the smallest year to year increase since March 1996 and the third consecutive monthly decline in the growth rate of the overall index. The charge-off rate averaged 5.57 percent during the third quarter, compared with 4.14 percent in the third quarter of 1995 and 5.52 percent in the second quarter of 1995. Moody's also indicated that the slowing pace in the charge-off growth rate reflected tighter standards and strengthened collection practices by the credit card lenders since early this year (*New York Times*, 1996b, p.D4).

The cyclical trends associated with consumer credit spending are interlinked with the pressures of everyday life and the need for enhanced buying power. The last major section deals with consumer credit and the quality of life from a postmodern economic perspective.

CONSUMER DEBT AND THE QUALITY OF LIFE

Credit cards and other forms of installment debt are the answer for consumers struggling with everyday financial obligations, low savings, and continual material needs. The quality-of-life issue is more dynamic because consumer credit and credit card facilitation of everyday life are linked with larger political, economic, and cultural factors. According to Stuart Hall (1991), the problem takes on a distinctly socio-political dimension. Hall claims that there is "an enormous expansion of 'civil society,' caused by the diversification of the different social worlds in which men and women can operate." He states that most people can only relate to these worlds through the "medium of consumption." Stuart postulates that these worlds self-contain their own codes of behavior, individual characteristics, and "pleasures." Our social selves are allowed space wherein we can "reassert a measure of choice and control over everyday life and to play with its more expressive dimensions." As a result, consumption of everyday life "expands the roles and identities available to ordinary people" (pp. 57–64).

The socio-economic perspective related to consumption and quality of life is also reflected in Harvey's (1991) analysis. Harvey conveys a clearer explanation of "Fordist" and "flexible" accumulation and ties the debate into a consideration of cultural life and political organization with "the relationship between modernist and postmodernist ways of thinking and of cultural production" (pp. 65–77).

Harvey sees flexibility as a condition in everyday life. Levels of flexibility include flexibility in relation to labor processes (speeding up labor processes and production of goods), labor market flexibility (new types of positions and subcontracting), state policy (deregulation and privatization), and flexibility in geographic mobility (relocation of the workplace) (pp. 70–72).

All of these relate to consumer culture because there is a new quality of life associated with the production and consumption of commodities purchased by consumers. The economic relations alter family structure, consumption patterns, or working conditions, while the cultural patterns dictate the formation of cultural capital. The impact of culturally filtered information is important in dictating the formation of a professional class emphasizing economic activity for the consumption of cultural capital. Harvey draws an important linkage relating the growth of service sector employment and the vast importance of media and culture forces. Cultural activities are democratized and filtered down into mass society. The "cultural mass" (or people working in the teaching and production of cultural expression) shapes the ongoing political, social, and economic contexts (p. 68).

The concern with culture and the flexibility built into the post-Fordist system inevitably give rise to an emerging postmodern movement. Harvey claims that postmodernism emphasizes the cultural mass, wherein taste, gentrification, and lifestyles are promoted through advertisements, film, architecture, music and other sources (pp. 73–77).

There are three levels in Harvey's analysis of postmodernism: (1) The production of images is an important facet of the reproduction and transformation of a social order; (2) a lack of focus on the larger consumer society and more inner directed emphasis on pluralistic notions are evident; and (3) there is a reordering of our sense of time and space (telecommunications and mass tourism change how we think the world works) (pp. 74–76).

All three are valid in a continual shift from the general to a specific interpersonal view of everyday life. Consumer credit and the commodities associated with consumer culture (and the cultural capital of everyday experience) are shaped by free-floating images. Credit cards enable us to go everywhere; and, in the words of a popular Visa credit card commercial, "We're everywhere you want to be."

Harvey pinpoints a crucial socio-economic pattern in the relationship between enhanced production and visible consumption (and, by inference, consumer credit) patterns. He interlinks the important relationship between postmodernism and consumer activity. Harvey points out that the speed-up in production is interlinked with flexibility. The process must also incorporate a related emphasis on enhancing marketing and banking in support of increased consumption.

Postmodernism is an important element in the overall process. Harvey claims that postmodernism concurrently reduces the acceptance of fashions and fads and emphasizes the production of images. Consumers can immediately act on commodity suggestions. The ultimate result encourages increased consumption and a greater consumer access to available goods and services (p. 76).

Production, consumption, and the transformation from cultural capital into economic capital are inevitably part of a larger structure. By inference, consumer credit and credit cards go beyond niche marketing in facilitating planning, calculated marketing decisions, and emphasis on leisure or style of life.[2] Immediate consumption of ideas or experiences is equal to or more powerful than the acquisition of material commodities.

SUMMARY AND CONCLUSIONS

Consumer credit and the generation of consumer debt represent a powerful force in American society. The present day acceptance of consumer debt for the acquisition of material goods, services, and experiences (such as travel and tourism) is an antithesis of thrift as a culturally accepted ideological value. Bankruptcy (or failure to repay one's debts) is less perceived as an inert character flaw than as a natural consequence of the contemporary consumer society. Credit cards are systematically marketed, and acquisitive consumer behavior (often as conspicuous consumption) is an everyday reality in capitalist societies. The "conferring" of a credit card is both a sign of status recognition and indispensable for "getting the most out of life."

Young adults, women, professional and occupational workers, and stratified social class groups all have access to credit cards and instant consumer gratification. The world is rapidly changing, the images speed across our eyes, and consumer culture enables us to "go with the flow." Alvin Toffler's (1973) vision of future shock was not far from the truth.[3] The credit card enables us to purchase images, ideas, material commodities signifying actual or anticipatory social status, and a cultural heritage through our travel experiences. Henry Ford was right: Cultural values and social class are the real commodities manufactured and purchased by a nation of workers and consumers.

We are living in a transformed society: The postindustrial society has given way to further differentiation, niche marketing and flexibility, and an ever shifting social order. Consumer credit has accomplished the institutionalization of consumerism. The shift from living within one's means into an ever changing society has yielded less permanence and more dependence on economic purchasing power in achieving everyday goals.

The gradual shift from a credit card society to an ATM society and eventually to an electronic funds transfer system-driven society operated by "smart cards" (containing data regarding our personal lives) will further ensure instant gratification through immediate purchasing power. Telephone sex, fantasy suites, and a Las Vegas vacation are all components of the consumer society. We can now expand the quality of our lives through the use of credit cards. Future technology will provide impetus for even more products, services, and experiences translatable from cultural capital into economic capital.

The advertising industry and commodity distribution networks continue to market (or shape) the consumed images and immediately make them available to a waiting public. Credit card advertisements convey the images that both encourage both consumer credit use and the desire for acquisition of commodities offered through retailing outlets. Cable television home shopping services and spectacular retailing showcases like the Mall of America feed into Herbert Marcuse's (1964) claim that we achieve identity through material possessions.

How can we characterize the importance of the consumer credit apparatus? Our society is in an ever evolving state of change. Consumer credit and the immediate utilization of credit cards help us cope with the continuing pressures of everyday life. We can "charge" admission to a famous theme park or for a fantasy suite or borrow cash at a Las Vegas casino as we pursue our own "field of dreams." Credit cards can also help us maintain a professional image or purchase the education and tools we need for ascending into a higher socio-economic status. But credit cards are dangerous if misused. The Descartian phrase "Fools with tools are still fools" is operative here.

Credit cards and other forms of consumer credit are a permanent fixture in American society. The institutionalization of consumerism is an evolving process. Postmodern thinkers tell us that everything is imagery, there is no certainty, and the structural grounding between socio-economic relationships and the lives of American consumers is always changing. What are the inevitable socio-economic implications of the consumer culture that was initiated in the early 1920s and continually develops innovative symbolic and material commodities for personal acquisition? Zukin (1991), Harvey (1989, 1991), and other seminal thinkers give us some clues. But inevitably the future of the relationship between the economic system and social values still "lies in the cards."

NOTES

1. Reported on a November 7, 1996 newscast by WTNH-TV, Channel 8, New Haven.

2. MacCannell (1989) renders some of these points in a specific analysis of tourism as a commodity

3. Toffler (1971) wrote about the rapid transformation of popular culture and the relationship between personal adjustment and rapid social change. We can now argue that the credit card is not merely a financial instrument: The symbolic value of a consumer's purchasing power facilitates continued adjustment through purchase of the symbolic goods or material possessions. Lefebvre (1971) was correct: the components of everyday life encompass consumer commodities.

Bibliography

Adorno, Theodor. 1973. *Negative Dialectics*. New York: Continuum.

Agnew, Robert. 1987. "Home Shopping: TV's Hit of the Season." *Marketing News*, 21, 6 (March 13): 1320.

Aronson, Sidney. 1979. "The Sociology of the Telephone." In *Inter-Media: Interpersonal Communication in a Media World*. Gary Gumpert and Robert Cathcart (eds.), pp. 126–136. New York: Oxford University Press.

Arts and Entertainment Network. 1993. *Gambling in America*. Hosted by Bill Kurtis. Broadcast on April 9.

Avery, Robert K., and Donald G. Ellis. 1979. "Talk Radio as an Interpersonal Phenomenon." In *Inter-Media: Interpersonal Communication in the Modern World*. Gary Gumpert and Robert Cathcart (eds.), pp. 108–116. New York: Oxford University Press.

Ball, Richard, and Robert Lilly. 1983. "No Tell Motel: The Management of Social Invisibility." In *Social Interaction: Readings in Sociology*. Howard Robboy and Candace Clark (eds.), pp. 165–176. New York: St. Martin's Press.

Bass, Jay Jacqueline. 1977. "Redefinition of Self in a Social Labeling Situation: A Social Psychological Investigation into the World of Default Debtors." Ph.D. dissertation, Michigan State University.

Bass, Jay Jacqueline. 1981. "The Sociology of Consumer Debt Collection." *Journal of Contemporary Ethnography*, 11, 2 (April): 124–164.

Baudrillard, Jean. 1983. *Simulations*. New York: Semiotext.

Bell, Daniel. 1953. "Crime as an American Way of Life."*Antioch Review* 13 (June): 125–145.

Bell, Daniel. 1976a. *The Coming of Post Industrial Society*. New York: Basic Books.

Bell, Daniel. 1976b. *The Cultural Contradictions of Capitalism*. New York: Basic Books.

Bellah, Robert, Richard Madsen, William Sullivan, Ann Swidler, and Steven Tipton. 1985. *Habits of the Heart*. Berkeley: University of California Press.

Bellah, Robert, Richard Madsen, William Sullivan, Ann Swidler, and Steven Tipton. 1991. *The Good Society*. Berkeley: University of California Press.

Bensman, Joseph. 1971. *The New American Society*. Chicago: Quadrangle.

Bensman, Joseph. 1973. *Craft and Consciousness*. New York: Wiley.

Bluestone, Barry and Bennett Harrison. 1982. *The Deinstitutionation of America: Plant Closings, Community Abandonment, and the Dismantling of Basic Industry*. New York: Basic Books.

Blumler, Jay, and Elihu Katz. 1974. *The Uses of Mass Communications*. Beverly Hills: Sage.

Bourdieu, Pierre. 1984. *Distinction: A Social Critique of the Judgment of Taste*. Cambridge, MA: Harvard University Press.

Braverman, Harry. 1975. *Labor and Monopoly Capital*. New York: Monthly Review Press.

Bryant, Adam. 1992. "Raising the Stakes in a War on Plastic." *New York Times*, September 13, p. D2.

Cable Network News. 1988. Business Week segment on the credit card industry, November 12.

Caplovitz, David. 1965. *The Poor Pay More: Consumer Practices of Low Income Families*. New York: Free Press.

Caplovitz, David. 1974. *Consumers in Trouble: A Study of Debtors in Default*. New York: Free Press.

Chicago Tribune. 1986. "Romper Rooms: Each Key Unlocks a Fantasy at the Dillon Royale Hotel." by Paul Galloway, October 1, Tempo Section, p. D2.

Cocheo, Steve. 1991. "Tackling Soaring Bankruptcy Filings." *ABA Banker Journal*, Volume 83, No. 3, March, 140–144.

Collins, Randall. 1982. *The Credentialed Society*. New York: Random House.

Dallas Morning News. 1987. "Hotel Offers Lodging Fit for a Fantasy." Bob Garfield, Today Section, May 5.

Dauten, Carl. 1956. *Financing the American Consumer*. St. Louis: American Investment Co. of Illinois.

Donahue, Phil. 1988. Televised discussion of cosmetics and beauty. Multimedia Productions.

Durkheim, Emile. 1910/1964. *The Division of Labor in Society*. New York: Free Press.

Edelstein, Alex S. 1993. "Thinking About the Criteria Variable in Agenda-Setting Research." *Journal of Communication* 43, 2 (Spring): 85–99.

Ehrenreich, Barbara. 1990. *Fear of Falling: The Inner Life of the Middle Class*. New York: HarperCollins.

Elliott, Stuart. 1993. Advertising column item entitled "Mastercard Tries to Change Its Image in a Campaign by Ammirati." *New York Times*, February 25, D7.

Esty, William. 1983. Interview with MasterCard account executive.

Ewen, Stuart. 1976. *Captains of Consciousness: Advertising and the Social Roots of the Consumer Culture*. New York: McGraw-Hill.

Ewen, Stuart. 1988. *All Consuming Images.* New York: Basic Books.

Ewen, Stuart and Elizabeth Ewen. 1982. *Channels of Desire.* New York: McGraw Hill.

Feagin, Joe. 1982. *Building Capitalist Cities: Developers, Bankers, Consumers.* Englewood Cliffs, N.J.: Prentice-Hall.

Featherstone, Mike. 1990. "Perspectives on American Culture." *Society,* 24, 1 (February): 34–48.

Featherstone, Mike. 1991. *Consumer Culture and Postmodernism.* Newbury Park, CA: Sage.

Federal Reserve Board. 1988. "Development in the US Financial System since the Mid-1970s." Thomas D. Simpson. *Monthly Labor Review,* 74, 1: 1–13.

Fitzgerald, Kate. 1990. "Card Issuers Poised to Fight Attorney." *Advertising Age,* 61, 27 (July 2): 12.

Forum Mall. 1993. Caesar's Palace media kit. December.

Foucault, Michel. 1984. *Discipline and Punish.* Harmondsworth: Penguin.

Freud, Sigmund. 1914. *Psychopathology of Everyday Life.* London: Benn.

Galbraith, John Kenneth. 1975. *The Affluent Society.* Boston: Houghton Mifflin.

Gartman, David. 1991. "Culture as Class Symbolization or Mass Reification? A Critique of Bourdieu's Distinction." *American Journal of Sociology,* 97, 2: 421–447.

Giddens, Anthony. 1987. *Social Theory and the Modern Society.* Stanford, CA: Stanford University Press.

Gitlin, Todd. 1983. *Inside Prime Time.* New York: Pantheon.

Goffman, Erving. 1959. *The Presentation of Self in Everyday Life.* New York. Anchor.

Goffman, Erving. 1971. *Relations in Public: Microstudies of Public Order.* New York: Basic Books.

Goffman, Erving. 1981. *Frame Analysis.* New York: McGraw Hill.

Gruen, Victor. 1973. *Centers for the Urban Environment: Survival of the Cities.* New York: Van Nostrand Reinhold Company.

Habermas, Jurgen. 1971. *Toward a Rational Society.* London: Heineman.

Hall, Stuart. 1991. "Brave New World." *Socialist Review,* Volume 21, No. 1 (January-March): 59–64.

Harvey, David. 1989. *The Condition of Postmodernity.* Boston: Blackwell.

Harvey, David. 1991. "Flexibility: Threat or Opportunity?" *Socialist Review,* 21, 1 (January-March): 65–77.

Hawk, Kathleen. 1988. "Don't Touch That Dial, This Time, Banks and Other Financial Providers Will Reach Out to Armchair Shoppers through the TV Set." *US Banker* 998 (April): 26–28.

Heinlein, Robert. 1959. *Stranger in a Strange Land.* New York: Putnam.

Hendrickson, Robert. 1974. *The Cashless Society.* New York: Dodd and Mead.

Hirsch, Fred. 1976. *The Limits to Growth.* Cambridge, MA: Harvard University Press.

Horkheimer, Max and Theodor Adorno. 1972. *Dialectic of Enlightenment.* New York: Herder and Herder.

Jacobs, Jerry. 1984. *The Mall: An Attempted Escape from Everyday Life.* Prospect Heights, IL: Waveland Press.

Jhally, Sut. 1987. *The Codes of Advertising.* New York: St. Martin's Press.

Jhally, Sut, and William Leiss. 1986. *Social Communication in Advertising*. Toronto: Methuen.

Johnson, Robert. 1980. "Credit in Retailing: Origins and Trends." In *Changing Universe of Consumer Credit: Issues and Developments in Periods*. New York: New York University.

Klein, Lloyd. 1983. "Sexual Encounters of the Fantasy Kind: Telephone Sex and Criminal Justice Concerns." Paper presented at the annual meeting of the Society for the Study of Social Problems, Detroit, MI.

Klein, Lloyd. 1990. "How Suite It Is: Specialty Hotel Rooms and Manufactured Sensuality" Paper Presented at the Annual Meeting of the Society for the Study of Social Problems, Washington, DC.

Klein, Lloyd, and Eva Bronstein-Greenwald. 1985. "Lifestyles of the Downwardly Mobile and Debtridden." Paper presented at the annual meeting of the American Sociological Association, Washington, DC.

Klein, Lloyd, and Joan Luxenburg. 1981. "Sex Solicitation by Short Wave Radio." *Free Inquiry in Creative Sociology*. 9, 1: 35–39.

Klein, Lloyd, and Joan Luxenburg. 1983. "CB Radio Prostitution: Technology and the Displacement of Deviance." *Journal of Offender Counseling, Services and Rehabilitation*, 9, 1: 20–24.

Klein, Philip A. 1971. "The Cyclist Timing of Consumer Credit, 1920–1967." *Occasional Paper 113, National Bureau of Economic Research*. New York: Columbia University Press.

Kosichu, Gerald M. 1993. "Problems and Opportunities in Agenda Setting Research." *Journal of Communication* 43, 2 (Spring): 100–127.

Lasch, Christopher. 1978. *Narcissism in American Society*. Englewood Cliffs, New Jersey: Prentice-Hall.

Lefebvre, Henri. 1971. *Everyday Life in the Modern World*. London: Allan Lane.

Leiss, William. 1978. *The Limits to Growth*. London: Marian Boyers. Leiss, William, Sut Jhally, and Steve Kline. 1986. *Social Construction in Advertising: Persons, Products and Images of Well-being*. Toronto: Methuen.

Lowenthal, Leo. 1948. *Literature and the Change of Man*. Boston, MA: Beacon.

Luckett, Charles A. 1988. "Personal Bankruptcies." *Federal Reserve Bulletin*, September, pp. 591–603.

Lyotard, Jean Francois. 1984. *The Postmodern Condition: A Report on Knowledge*. Minneapolis: University of Minnesota Press.

MacCannell, Dean. 1989. *The Tourist: A New Theory of the Leisure Class*. New York: Schocken Books.

Mandell, Louis. 1990. *The Credit Card Industry: A History*. Boston, MA: Twayne.

Marcuse, Herbert. 1964. *One-Dimensional Man*. Cambridge: Routledge and Kegan-Paul.

Marx, Karl. 1860/1967. *Capital: A Critique of Political Economy*. New York: International Publishers.

MasterCard, Inc. 1993. Affiliate marketing package surrounding the "Mastercard-Smart Money" campaign.

McCombs, Maxwell E., and Donald L. Shaw. 1993. "The Evolution of Agenda Setting Research: Twenty-Five Years in the Marketplace of Ideas." *Journal of Communication* 43, 2 (Spring): 58–67.

McGovern, Gary. 1987. "A Social History of Economic Development." Paper presented at the annual meeting of the Eastern Sociological Society, Boston, MA.

Merton, Robert K. 1968. *Social Theory and Social Structure*. Glencoe, IL: Free Press.

Mirage Hotel and Casino. 1993. Press release materials. February.

Morality in Media, Inc. 1984. Comment submitted to the Federal Communications Commission on "Inquiry into and Proposed Rulemaking Regarding Enforcement of Prohibitions against the Use of Common Carriers for the Transmission of Obscene Materials," Docket No. 83–989.

Natanson, Maurice, ed. 1964. *Phenomenology and the Social Reality: Essays in the Memory of Alfred Schutz*. The Hague: Nijhoff.

National Retail Merchants Association. 1986. Interview with an associate director.

Neal, Charles. 1967. *Sense with Dollars*. Rev. paperback ed. Garden City, NY: Doubleday.

New York Times. 1982. Special section on anti-trust legislation and telecommunications. January 9: 34–37.

New York Times. 1988. "In Midwest Hotels, Choose Igloos or Pharaoh's Tomb," by William E. Schmidt. October 13, III, p. 1.

New York Times. 1992. "Bankruptcy Filing at 47th Street Photo," by Stephanie Strom. January 22, p. D1.

New York Times. 1996a. "Default Rate Up for Consumers." November 8, p. D4.

New York Times. 1996b "Consumer Borrowing Pace Declined during September," by Robert D. Hershey Jr. November 8, p. D4.

O'Connor, James. 1973. *The Fiscal Crisis of the State*. New York: St. Martin's Press.

O'Connor, James. 1982. *Accumulation Crisis*. New York: Basil Blackwell.

Ogilvy and Mather. 1992. American Express advertising print advertising and videotaped television commericals.

Philadelphia Inquirer. 1983. "Her Ventures Are the X Rated Kind." July 15, pp. E1, E4.

Piore, Michael, and Charles Sable. 1984. *The Second Industrial Divide: Possibilities for Prospects*. New York: Basic Books.

Polenberg, Michael. 1980. *National Divide*. New York: Viking Press.

Potter, David. 1954. *People of Plenty: Economic Abundance and the American Character*. Chicago: University of Chicago Press.

Povich, Maury. 1993. Segment on telepsychics. Paramount Productions, February.

Public Broadcasting Service. 1989. American Experience: Sears Retail Business. October.

Public Broadcasting Service. 1992. Adam Smith's Money World: program on credit cards. November.

Reich, Charles. 1970. *The Greening of America: How the Youth Revolution Is Trying to Make America Liveable*. New York: Random House.

Reisman, David, Nathan Glazer, and Reuel Denney. 1950. *The Lonely Crowd: A Study of the Changing American Character*. New Haven, CT: Yale University Press.

Richard, Steven. 1983. "The Business of Pornography in an Adult Bookstore." Paper presented at the annual meeting of the Society for the Study of Social Problems, Detroit, MI.

Ritzer, George. 1993. *The McDonaldization of Society*. Newbury Park, CA: Pine Forge Press.

Rogers, Everett M., James W. Dearing, and Dorine Bregman. 1993. "The Analysis of Agenda-Setting Research." *Journal of Communication*, 43, 2 (Spring): pp. 68–84.

Rule, James, Douglas McAdam, Linda Stearns, and David Uglow. 1980. *The Politics of Privacy*. New York: Mentor.

Rybczynski, Witold. 1993. "The New Downtowners." *Atlantic Monthly*, 271, 5: 98–106.

Schor, Juliet. 1991. *The Overworked American: The Unexpected Decline of Leisure*. New York: Basic Books.

Schor, Juliet. 1998. *The Overspent American*. New York: Basic Books.

Schudson, Michael. 1984. *Advertising: The Uneasy Persuasion*. New York: Harper.

Smith, Robert Ellis. 1980. *Privacy: How to Protect What's Left of It*. New York: Anchor Doubleday.

Smock, Robert. 1962. "Social Change and Personal Debt: A Historical Introduction to the Sociology of Consumer Credit." Ph.D. dissertation, Wayne State University.

Sullivan, Teresa, Elizabeth Warren, and Jay Lawrence Westbrook. 1989. *As We Forgive Our Debtors: Bankruptcy and Consumer Credit in America*. New York: Oxford University Press.

Time. 1983. "Splitting AT&T." November 21, pp. 25–26.

Time. 1984. "Sex in the '80s: The Revolution Is Over." April 19, pp. 32–33.

Toffler, Alvin. 1973. *Future Shock*. New York: Bantam Books.

Touraine, Alain. 1971. *The Post Industrial Society; Tomorrow's Social History: Classes, Conflicts and Culture in the Programmed Society*. New York: Random House.

U.S. Bureau of the Census. 1978. *Statistical Abstract of the United States*. Washington, DC: U.S. Government Printing Office.

Urry, John. 1990. "The 'Consumption' of Tourism." *Sociology*, 24, 1: 90–96.

Veblen, Thorstein. 1899/1983. *Theory of the Leisure Class*. New York: Penguin.

Visa, Inc. 1982. Visa Consumer Marketing Plan.

Walt Disney Organization. 1993. Training manual.

Webb, James. 1983. Interview at American Express Company.

Weber, Max. 1902/1958. *The Protestant Ethic and the Spirit of Capitalism*. Translated by Talcott Parsons. New York: Free Press.

Weber, Max. 1946. "Class, Status, and Power." In *From Max Weber*. New York: Free Press.

Wilson, William Julius. 1991. "Studying Inner-City Social Dislocations." *American Sociological Review*, 56, No. 1 (February): 1–14. ASA Presidential Address delivered at the annual meeting of the American Sociological Association, Washington, DC, August 1990.

Winick, Charles and Paul Kinsie. 1971. *The Lively Commerce: Prostitution in the United States*. Chicago: Quadrangle.

Zukin, Sharon. 1990. "Socio-Spatial Prototypes of a New Organization of Consumption: The Role of Real Cultural Capital." *Society*, 24, 1, February: 34–55.

Zukin, Sharon. 1991. *Landscapes of Power: From Detroit to Disney World*. Berkeley: University of California Press.

Zukin, Sharon, and Paul DiMaggio. 1990. *Structures of Capital: The Social Organization of the Economy*. Boston: Cambridge University Press.

Index

About the Author

LLOYD KLEIN is Associate Professor of Sociology at Medgar Evers College, CUNY. His research has focused on the areas of social economy, mass media, criminal justice, and deviant behavior.

ISBN 0-275-95757-8

HARDCOVER BAR CODE